PQ 3989.2.K3.2S
1T

Critical Guides to French Texts

127 Cheikh Hamidou Kane: L'Aventure ambiguë

Critical Guides To French Texts

EDITED BY ROGER LITTLE, WOLFGANG VAN EMDEN, DAVID WILLIAMS

CHEIKH HAMIDOU KANE

L'Aventure ambiguë

J. P. Little

Lecturer in French,
St Patrick's College, Dublin

Grant & Cutler Ltd
2000

© Grant & Cutler Ltd 2000

ISBN 0 7293 0425 6

DEPÓSITO LEGAL: V. 4.643 - 2000

Printed in Spain by
Artes Gráficas Soler, S.A., Valencia
for
GRANT & CUTLER LTD
55-57 GREAT MARLBOROUGH STREET, LONDON W1V 2AY

Contents

To the Diallobé of Ndiébène Toubé

Prefatory Note

Reference for *L'Aventure ambiguë* is made to the paperback, Union Générale d'Editions, Coll. 10/18, 1971, and frequently reprinted, most recently in 1999. Other works are referred to by italicised number, cross-referenced to the Select Bibliography. Where no italicised number appears, reference is to *L'Aventure ambiguë*. Where there is a succession of references to the same page, the first only is given. My more general debt to writers working in the many areas covered in this study has, for reasons of space, had to be restricted to those listed in the bibliography. An expanded version of Chapter I is due to appear in *Research in African Literatures*.

For the anglicised forms of Pular terms, I have followed those adopted by David Robinson in *68*, Appendix I: (Glossary). For French forms in quotations, I have retained those used by the author in question.

I should like to acknowledge most warmly the assistance given me in the writing of this monograph by Cheikh Hamidou Kane, who granted me several interviews, and whose general availability was a source of great encouragement to me. I would also extend sincere thanks to members of his family in Matam, Saldé and Dakar, for their generous and spontaneous hospitality, and for their patience in answering questions. The help of other friends and colleagues, notably in Senegal, who have also contributed in their several ways, but who are too numerous to mention individually, is again to be acknowledged most sincerely. Finally I would thank my husband, Roger, whose encouragement and support have been unfailing throughout, and who experienced with me some of the unforgettable moments which went into the writing of this volume.

J. P. L.

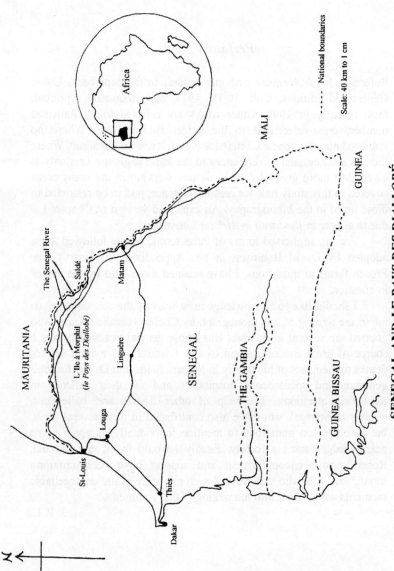

SENEGAL AND *LE PAYS DES DIALLOBÉ*

1. Autofiction

Cheikh Hamidou Kane belongs to a whole generation of Francophone African writers who felt the need to give an account in fictionalised form of their intellectual itinerary. This exploration invariably involves a clash of cultures, with the 'new school', *l'école des Blancs*, introduced by the colonising power acting as catalyst in the transition from the traditional world of the African village to the wider world influenced by European values, frequently represented by a crucially formative period spent in Paris. Sometimes the emphasis is on the lost childhood world, and the Paris period mostly implicit, as in what is probably the most famous of these novels of childhood, Laye Camara's *L'Enfant noir* (1953); sometimes Paris is foregrounded to convey dramatically the psychological trauma caused by contact with an alien world: Ousmane Socé's *Mirages de Paris* (1937) or Aké Loba's *Kokoumba, l'étudiant noir* (1960) spring to mind in this context, or Mudimbe's *L'Ecart* (1979); sometimes it is the alienating effect of school itself that is emphasised, and the disrupting effect it has on the families involved, as in Seydou Badian's *Sous l'orage* (1963). In all these novels, the autobiographical element, while exploited differently, is crucial. An analysis of Cheikh Hamidou Kane's use of autobiographical material in the structuring of *L'Aventure ambiguë* (1961), will also allow a broader perspective on what this material actually comprises.

General considerations of form remind us that African prose fiction can be difficult to classify, if only because the novel does not exist as such in the African oral tradition. Mohamadou Kane, as long ago as 1975, deplored the European critic's apparent need to classify at all costs, even if classification discounted the tradition from which the form arose (*57*, p.16). Autobiography is by general agreement purely European in origin, and its absence from the African tradition is entirely understandable in the context of the collective, non-individualistic nature of African culture. Referring to the very profession of the writer, Cheikh Hamidou Kane himself notes that:

> Le métier d'écrivain n'existait pas dans nos cultures, et à
> plus forte raison, on n'a pas de poètes, de romanciers et
> de mémorialistes. Tout cela, ce sont des formes, des
> genres qui sont liés à la pratique de l'écriture. Chez moi,
> ce qui existe c'est la parole, c'est le conte, c'est la
> légende, c'est le proverbe, etc., c'est le dialogue. (*16*)

The author's own definition, *récit*, appears on the title page, a
definition which can be justified in particular regarding the discretion
and lack of direct involvement in the narrative on the part of the
narrator, as well as the narrator's perspective, necessitating the use of
passé simple and pluperfect (*20*, p.57). For the purposes of this study
I shall be retaining the nearest English equivalent, 'novel', but Kane's
choice of the term *récit* can be seen as one of a number of distancing
devices, which brings us immediately to the relationship between the
author and the literary work produced.

Any consideration of autobiography or autofiction requires the
assessment, among other things, of the relationship between the
author and the narrator, and the author and the main character of the
fiction. There is an argument to be made, of course, for the idea that
all creative writing engages the writer in an autobiographical sense,
and is revealing of the intimate self of that writer. But in a more
technical sense, for a work to be a true autobiography, there must be
identity between author, narrator and main character. (For general
considerations of autobiography, see the writings of Philippe Lejeune
and Georges Gusdorf, among others.) In the case of *L'Aventure
ambiguë*, as in Bernard Dadié's *Climbié*, the use of the third-person
narrative suggests, though does not prove, a distancing of author and
principal character: a more telling proof of this distance lies in the
fact that the principal character dies towards the end of the novel. The
only way a first-person narrative could have been sustained therefore
would have been through the discovery (by the narrator) of a first-
person diary, as in Oyono's *Une Vie de boy* (1956), for example, or
some such other artifice, and this would still not have established
identity between author and main character.

There would thus seem to have been a deliberate decision on
the part of Kane to distance himself from his creation. It would

appear to be maintained in the choice of name, Samba Diallo, for his main character. But here the matter immediately becomes more ambiguous, since Samba Diallo is in fact another name for Cheikh Hamidou Kane. By virtue of his being the second son of his family, he received the conventional forename Samba (he is still referred to thus within the family); Diallo is the Fula equivalent of the Tokolor name Kane. I shall return to this latter point, but it seems to indicate already that Kane wanted both to be and not to be Samba Diallo.

Some light may perhaps be thrown on the relationship by looking into the origins of what Kane calls the *récit*. It has always been known that the fictionalised version we now have started life as a *Journal intime*, written during the end of his studies at the Lycée Van Vollenhoven and the Institut des Hautes Etudes de Dakar, but mostly in Paris (see e.g. *17*, p.4 and *13*, p.479). Kane regretted in interview that this *Journal* had not survived, as it would have given a precious indication of the path leading from day-to-day reflection on the development of a consciousness to the final fiction (*16*). He also, interestingly, confessed that he could no longer remember whether the *Journal* was written in the first or third person, leaving open the possibility that the distancing process was already at work. He is, however, quite clear as to his motivation in keeping the *Journal*:

> Effectivement, quand j'ai commencé à rédiger ce qui devait être *L'Aventure ambiguë,* je ne l'avais pas fait dans l'intention d'écrire une œuvre romanesque, ou même de rédiger des mémoires. Je n'avais pas entrepris de le faire dans l'intention de répondre à l'un des genres littéraires qui étaient pratiqués en Europe. [...] La seule chose qui m'avait inspiré, c'était le souci de mettre noir sur blanc ce qui m'advenait dans ce passage [...] d'une société traditionnelle, appartenant à une culture orale, à une société moderne, dont le medium principal est l'écriture. C'est ce passage qui a été si étonnant, si extraordinaire que, au fur et à mesure que je suivais ce parcours, j'ai été amené à noter des impressions, des moments importants, des interrogations, des réponses que j'apportais à ces interrogations [...] donc c'est cela qui avait fourni la

matière d'un document [...] qui était comme une sorte de
journal intime.

The motive in keeping the *Journal* in the first place was thus
largely one of recording what seemed to him to be the extraordinary
nature of his experience, plus, no doubt, the process of self-discovery
and even self-creation through writing, common to late adolescence
and early adulthood. (Kane goes further, indeed, when he says that
his whole life has been '[la] poursuite en usant de l'écriture de
l'expression de mon identité propre', *15*.) The *Journal* ended,
however, when Kane finished his studies in Paris, so that the whole of
the final part devoted to Samba Diallo's return to the *pays des
Diallobé* is a fictional creation. The decision to extend the *Journal* in
this way and to publish it came later, after Kane's own return to
Senegal in 1958, on the advice of friends, one of whom was Vincent
Monteil, who wrote the Preface to the first edition, and who felt that
the writing would interest a wider public. Kane has recorded on
several occasions the reasons for the passage from the early
manuscript to publication (e.g. *13*, p.480), emphasising the
importance of witness: as he says,

> au moment où j'écrivais [...] c'était un peu pour donner
> un témoignage aux Occidentaux, de l'existence d'une
> culture, d'une civilisation, d'une sensibilité noire,
> puisque les Occidentaux ne pouvaient accéder à cette
> culture, à la connaissance de ces valeurs, et de cette
> sensibilité que par le moyen de l'écriture et des livres.
> [...] Nous, nous étions déjà voués à la démonstration de
> l'existence de valeurs et de culture à travers l'oralité,
> valeurs et culture qui étaient universelles et que nous
> pouvions partager avec les autres. (*16*)

There was also the desire, arising from the consciousness
already of the slow but steady loss of these values, to share them with
the next generation:

> Je crois qu'il y avait aussi un deuxième objectif, celui
> d'armer, d'outiller les générations africaines, pour
> informer les jeunes de l'existence de ces cultures, parce
> que, par ailleurs, nous étions mieux enracinés dans ces
> cultures traditionnelles que les jeunes générations.

There is therefore implicit in the writing a will to universalise.
Samba Diallo is seen from the beginning as exemplary, as speaking
for a whole generation, and the novel is not simply the recording of
one individual's development. The cultural motivation seems to have
been paramount.

What is it, then, to which Kane wishes to bear witness? In
terms of the geographical location of the story, the desire to render
his experience universal seems present from the outset in the
remarkable fact that, with the exception of Paris, not a single place is
named in the novel which can be identified on a map. Senegal itself is
never mentioned, the identity of the 'petite ville de L.', where Samba
Diallo goes to the French school, and which is in fact Louga, a small
town to the south-east of St Louis (*16*), is left deliberately mysterious,
while the *pays des Diallobé*, Kane's name for the historical province
of Yirlabé, simply refers back to Samba Diallo, the suffix *bé* (or more
properly *Be*) designating 'people' (as in *Burkinabé*, the people of
Burkina Faso). Far from rendering these places neutral, however, the
distancing device serves rather to give them mythical status. The *pays
des Diallobé*, when Samba Diallo is in Paris, is a kind of paradise
lost, from which he is now in exile. In Europe, as he says, 'je ne brûle
plus au cœur des êtres et des choses' (p.174), 'je vis moins
pleinement qu'au Pays des Diallobé' (p.162). This area with which
Samba Diallo feels such an intense bond is in reality the Ile à
Morphil, the long island created by the separation of the Senegal
River into two distinct branches, in the far north of the country,
owing its name to the hunting for ivory that went on there from the
mid-seventeenth century, when the French established a trading-post
in St Louis. At its south-eastern point lies Saldé, the colonial *chef-lieu
de canton*, and it is there, in the *foyer ardent*, that the novel opens. In
Samba Diallo's time, sixty years ago, the area abounded in wild
animals: panthers, lions and hyenas, but it was so isolated from the

rest of the country that to leave the area of the Futa Toro generally was to 'go down to Senegal'. Today, with increasing desertification, it is arid and depopulated, the inhabitants of its remaining scattered villages living out a precarious existence, largely ignored and forgotten, with poor infrastructure, and cut off from the rest of Senegal by unreliable, hand-operated ferries over the river. The state of its internal services is such that it is referred to locally as 'l'île à mort vite'. The West-East road link with the capital is still not viable, and access to the whole area of the Futa is via St Louis and the great curve of the Senegal River, a distance of some 700 kilometres from Dakar. As we see in *L'Aventure ambiguë*, however, this is the area which was capable of inspiring in Samba Diallo a fierce loyalty and a permanent nostalgia when once it is no longer physically present, a spiritual home, needing no descriptions of local colour to make it come alive. What is being evoked is a whole way of life, a culture going back centuries, under threat from the moment of the coloniser's arrival, through what the French perceived as their 'civilising mission', and increasingly fragile today, unable to maintain a viable tradition whilst benefiting only marginally, if at all, from the modern, technological culture which bears in upon it.

What are the characteristics of this society to which Cheikh Hamidou Kane wishes to bear witness? What are its origins and its place in Senegalese society? It might be appropriate at this point to give some indication of the roots to which Kane is so singularly attached. He and his family are of Tokolor origin, or *Hal-pulaar'en*, 'speakers of Pular', as they prefer to be known. The designation of Tokolor is a French corruption of Takruur, the old Arabic term dating from the tenth century for the area corresponding to the modern Futa Toro, which extends over the Senegalese and Mauritanian banks of the Senegal River between Bakel and Podor. The area was one of the earliest to come under the influence of Islam, a process which had probably started already in the eleventh century (see *63*, p.124). In the early sixteenth century control of the area was wrested from the Manding Empire of Mali by the Denyanke Fulbe, reputedly pagan, until, with the increasing influence of Islam they were overthrown in 1776 by the Tokolors, led by the fervently Muslim 'parti maraboutique' (*75*, pp.9-12), for ideological as much as for political reasons. In a society organised on a caste basis, their religious aristocracy, the *toorodbe* (the term means 'the people who pray together' (*50*, p.23) or 'beggars for alms' (*68*, p.177)) saw themselves as possessed of an evangelising mission. Through the dominant 'grandes familles', they also rapidly became a social and political aristocracy, exercising great power in the area which lasted throughout the colonial era, when the French, realising that they could not subdue this proud and independent-minded people, used them in their attempts at control of the region. Indeed, so resistant were they to direct control by the French, that the coloniser simply used the structures in place, and political organisation in the Futa resembled the 'indirect rule' of the British colonial regime (*48*, p.46). Hence, of course, the importance of the school, at the heart of *L'Aventure ambiguë*, as an indirect means of subduing the region. It is certain that the strong presence among the Tokolors of Islam, which formed an essential part of their identity, made the colonising mission of the French immeasurably more difficult, at the same time as it made the clash of cultures for those, like Samba Diallo, who were plucked from their indigenous culture and put through the French educational system, considerably more acute. There is a stability about Tokolor society which would make any sudden contact with the outside world doubly shocking. Yaya Wane characterises it as 'une société inégalitaire ou hiérarchique, sur fond de féodalisme structurel' (*76*, p.890), adding that 'la caractéristique majeure de la collectivité toucouleur c'est d'abord l'inégalité interpersonnelle érigée en système clos et immuable: inégalité des castes, des sexes comme des générations.' Vincent Monteil quotes a Fulbe poem, collected by Gilbert Vieillard, which illustrates well the immutable nature of that society:

> Chacun sa tâche, et qu'il s'y tienne!
> Pêcheur, replonge ton filet!
> Toi, Peul, garde ton troupeau!
> Nègre, conserve ta bêche!
> Forgeron, garde ton enclume:
> Pour habiter une bonne terre.
> Qu le clerc soit à ses planchettes,
> Tout le jour écrit ses versets! (etc.) (*62*, p.352)

Applied in an Islamic context, the notion of structured obedience became sacralised in the course of time, and vestiges of the old ethos, identified in the following quotation relating to the nineteenth century, are evident even today:

> La soumission de l'individu au groupe, la soumission familiale ou sociale dans la société toucouleur islamisée, ainsi que celle des personnes moins âgées aux plus âgées, sont réinterprétées comme une simple étape vers la soumission à Dieu. (*72*, p.127)

Samba Diallo accepts readily therefore both submission to his religious master, Maître Thierno, and also to his family: although saddened to be leaving his spiritual home that was the *foyer ardent*, he does not question the family decision that he should start to attend the French school, even though at that point he has no particular desire to enter a different system. Born into the caste of the *toorodbe*, he is destined to rule, even if, as a child, he finds this destiny weighs heavy on him at times, as when he is singled out for his origins:

> Tous les disciples savaient combien il lui déplaisait que soit fait cas de son origine patricienne. Assurément, il était le mieux né de tout le foyer du maître des Diallobé. Nul, dans ce pays, ne le lui laissait ignorer. Lorsqu'il mendiait sa nourriture et, comme ce matin, passait dans toutes les demeures, des plus humbles aux plus cossues, chacun, en lui apportant les restes pourris des repas, lui manifestait par un signe ou par un geste que sous ses haillons le pays reconnaissait et saluait déjà un de ses guides futurs. La noblesse de son origine lui pesait, non point comme un fardeau dont il eût peur, mais à la manière d'un diadème trop encombrant. (pp.26-27)

In this respect at least, Cheikh Hamidou Kane would seem to be evoking his own experience in the literary form of Samba Diallo. But his vision of the character he wishes to convey is remote from, for example, the individual, Romantic hero of earlier times. Samba

Diallo *is* the society he springs fro n, *is* the latest incarnation of a
family type going back generation . In a family in which the oral
tradition has been maintained mor or less intact, and in which the
genealogy is still recalled by the *griots*, Samba Diallo is integral to
his milieu.

The family today traces back its origins to the patriarch, Alpha
Ciré Diallo (Cheikh Hamidou Kane's paternal great-grandfather and
maternal great-great grandfather). To clarify the complexity, the
relevant part of the family tree is presented diagramatically on page
19 below. Through intermarriage, the family adopted the name Kane,
the Tokolor equivalent of Diallo -- hence the identity between Samba
Diallo and Cheikh Hamidou Kane. Two of Alpha Ciré's sons had
French schooling and careers with the colonial administration,
Abdoulaye in particular becoming *chef supérieur* of Yirlabé province
(the first *chef des Diallobé*), highly respected l both the colonial
powers and the local chiefs. He seems to have t en possessed of a
great sense of realism: accepting the superior strength of the French,
he realised that compromise was necessary if his traditional culture
was not simply to be wiped out. S

Speaking these days of his family, Kane is emphatic that the
attitude of Abdoulaye and others who compromised with the French
was not simply a sell-out, and underlines the role played by the
family in maintaining the traditional, largely Islamic culture. Another
son of Alpha Ciré's, also Cheikh Hamidou, was a Muslim judge in
Matam, a noted Sufi mystic who had a great influence on his
grandson. In terms both of French-style and Muslim education, the
family was responsible for the education of a large number of
families in the Futa. What is presented in *L'Aventure ambiguë*,
therefore, as a new debate on education, had in fact been going on
since the second half of the nineteenth century.

With the generation of Alpha Ciré's grandchildren, we find
characters who appear in various guises in *L'Aventure ambiguë*. One
of the sons of Cheikh Hamidou, the Muslim judge, was Cheikh
Hamidou Kane's father, Mamadou Lamine, *le Chevalier*, while
another grandchild, Binta Racine, appears as the formidable figure of
la Grande Royale. Any scepticism regarding the possibility of a
woman exercising the sort of power attributed to her in the novel is

dispelled by hearing the views of other members of her family: her brother, Hamidou Abdoulaye, who appears in the novel as the *chef des Diallobé*, did not defer to her merely out of weakness. The strong pragmatic sense of *la Grande Royale* seems also to have been present in the real person. Kane has thus created a number of strong literary portraits from the people he grew up with, but it is important to retain the context of the society from which they evolved. The *Maître des Diallobé, la Grande Royale, le Chevalier, le Chef*, are the last representatives of the aristocratic *toorodbe* leadership brought to power at the end of the eighteenth century, and *L'Aventure ambiguë* is 'above all a fictional reconstruction of the political and ideological palingenesis of Diallobé society from the *toorodbe* Islamic revolution of the late 18th century to the era of colonial domination' (*27*, pp.32-33).

This then is the family into which Cheikh Hamidou Kane was born, and which is evoked in more or less detail in *L'Aventure ambiguë*. To what extent, however, is Samba Diallo a faithful recreation of the writer? How close is the identity between the destiny of Samba Diallo as recounted in the novel, and that of the novelist? Since the events of the novel turn largely around the crucial issue of the boy's education, it could be instructive at this point to make a comparison between the respective routes their schooling took.

In the novel, Samba Diallo's religious education in the Koranic school begins at the *foyer ardent*, on the suggestion of the *Maître des Diallobé* himself (p.22). We are not told where the *foyer ardent* is, but understand that it is some distance away. In Cheikh Hamidou Kane's case, he begins his Koranic education in Louga, where his father is a functionary with the French administration, but remains there only a few months, before continuing (with *Thierno* Mustapha Hafiz Gadio, called the *maître des Diallobé* in the novel) in Saldé.[1] It

---

[1] Much of the following information on Cheikh Hamidou's schooling was communicated to me by the author himself in interview on 10 February 1998. Supplementary details supplied by the current *Directeur* of the *Ecole élémentaire mixte régionale I* in Louga, Alioune Badara Fall. There remains an ambiguity concerning the length of time the young Kane spent in Louga: whereas he himself recalls it as having been less than an academic year, the school records show it to have been from 3 November 1937 to 10 May 1941.

is clear that substantially the experience is the same, and Cheikh Hamidou Kane is evoking his own experience in that of Samba Diallo. After an unspecified period of time, however, the decision is taken by the Diallobé, initiated by *la Grande Royale*, to send Samba Diallo to the new *école étrangère*. The narrator does not specify where this is, but the reader subsequently discovers that it is in the 'petite ville de L.' At this point there is an abrupt break with the *foyer ardent*. In the case of Kane himself, things are slightly more complicated: at the age of ten, the decision is taken by the family, essentially again prepared by *la Grande Royale* (in real life Binta Racine, his aunt and grandmother in African parlance). The child was then sent to Louga, where his father was based, but since his father (as in the novel) still hesitated to take the step, some months passed before any action was taken, although he continued to attend the Koranic school. The final decision was precipitated by his uncle, Issa Kane, a schoolteacher in Matam, who happened to be passing through Louga on his way to Kédougou, where he was essentially being exiled after a disagreement with a French school inspector. Seeing the young 'Samba' not in school at a time when normally he should have been, he immediately took him there and registered him, thus initiating the boy's career with the *école étrangère*. Comparing the situation of Samba Diallo with that of Cheikh Hamidou Kane himself, two details seem important: in the novel Issa Kane plays no role, thus highlighting the importance of *la Grande Royale*; secondly, whereas Kane continues to attend the Koranic school, in Samba Diallo's case there is an abrupt break between the two systems, rendering much more dramatic the cultural confrontation which is at the heart of the novel. The fact that Samba Diallo manages, after a mere three years at the Koranic school, to perform for his parents the *nuit du Coran*, during which the whole Koran is recited by heart, is surprising, a considerable feat of memory, but by no means impossible according to his creator. The novel is lean, spare, concentrating on the essentials necessary to convey the drama and the pathos of Samba Diallo's predicament, and leaving aside the incidental complications of the real-life situation.

The same phenomenon is apparent when the subsequent real and fictionalised academic situations are compared. After three and a half years at school in Louga, Cheikh Hamidou Kane then finished his primary schooling in Matam, obtaining his *Certificat d'Etudes Primaires Elémentaire*, before continuing at the *Ecole Primaire Supérieure* in St Louis. This school was combined with the *Ecole des Fils de Chef*, in the sense that they had a common programme for three years, after which the *Ecole des Fils de Chef* added a further, fourth year, which Kane accomplished successfully. Wanting to take his studies further, but being refused permission to follow classes at the Lycée Faidherbe in St Louis, he worked by himself to be in a position, at great personal effort, to enter the Lycée Van Vollenhoven in Dakar in 1948. To continue to receive the bursary of which he had been the beneficiary at the *Ecole des Fils de Chef*, however, he was obliged to commit himself to working for the French administration for ten years after he had finished his studies, and this largely determined Cheikh Hamidou Kane's career.

Only the broadest outlines of this itinerary appear in the novel: we see Samba Diallo in primary school in 'L.', but the only indication of his passage through the secondary level lies in the conversation with his father, *le Chevalier*, in which Pascal is evoked (pp.106-18). We can suppose that this took place in Thiès, not far from Dakar, where his father had taken retirement. Again, the author's sureness of touch in streamlining events is admirable, in that all attention is focused on the issues, and on the debate which the situation gave rise to, rather than on incidental detail, which would have removed from that debate its universal quality.

In Dakar, Kane first opted for the *Baccalauréat Moderne*, but since his aim was to become a philosophy teacher, undertook also the *Bac Philosophie* and then a year's *Propédeutique en Lettres*. At the same time, however, the Colonial Administration required him to register for a *Licence en Droit*, as a condition of his bursary. But since Dakar did only one year of the Law Degree, he was obliged to go on to Paris to complete it. The same pattern of intense intellectual effort continued in Paris, where the young student was accepted into the Lycée Louis-le-Grand to prepare for the entrance examination to the 'Ecole Coloniale', the *Ecole de la France d'outre-mer*. After a year and a half at Louis-le-Grand, he put in a further two years' effort at the *Ecole de la France d'outre-mer* and at the Sorbonne, giving him at the end a full *Licence en Droit*, a *Diplôme en Droit*, and a *Licence en Philosophie*. He returned to Senegal in 1958 to take up a career in the Colonial Administration. It should be noted also that throughout the period in Dakar and in Paris, Cheikh Hamidou was politically active, being a founder member of the *Association des Elèves de Dakar*, where his militancy caused him to be threatened with the withdrawal of his bursary, and in Paris as a committed member of the *Fédération d'Etudiants d'Afrique Noire en France*.

Against this background, Samba Diallo seems rather to be the realisation of Cheikh Hamidou's inner life, a reflective, ardent soul with mystical leanings, whose ambition was to meditate on life's insoluble questions and (possibly) teach philosophy (p.124). We see him in Paris with Lucienne's family as a student of philosophy (2e Partie, ch. I): there is no mention of other studies he is undertaking (he tells Pierre-Louis quite specifically that he has never studied law, p.143), there are no problems with the French administration, and any political activity seems to be precluded. In the debate with Lucienne (2e Partie, ch. IV), it is she who is politically active, while Samba Diallo, already torn by internal debate, is more preoccupied with his relationship to the God of his childhood faith than with any form of militant activity. Samba Diallo at this point is indeed Cheikh Hamidou Kane, but one facet only of a rich and multiple personality.

With the end of Kane's studies in Paris, he parts company with Samba Diallo in any literal sense. Returning in 1958 at the very end of the colonial regime, he alternately occupied ministerial functions in the new Senegalese state, and held various major United Nations and UNESCO posts in the Ivory Coast, Nigeria and Canada. Samba Diallo returns to the *pays des Diallobé*, but is killed by the character known as *le fou* shortly afterwards, apparently in a misunderstanding caused by *le fou*'s deranged perception of Samba Diallo as the new *maître des Diallobé*. *Le fou* is an invention on the part of his author, although a clearly recognisable type, one of the many Africans, usually *Tirailleurs sénégalais*, whose mental equilibrium had been unhinged by their experience in Europe. *Le fou* creates a slight problem for the narrative sequence in the sense that we meet him for the first time on Samba Diallo's return; he does not appear to have known the young man previously, although he is clearly part of the community, as we first meet him in conversation with the *maître des Diallobé* at the end of Thierno's life, when Samba Diallo is in Paris. Yet it is hardly plausible that two notable characters from the same small village should have been unaware of each other's existence. In considering autobiographical elements in the novel, what Cheikh Hamidou Kane now has to say on Samba Diallo's death is full of interest. We shall return to this crucial topic in chapter 5 below, but it is useful at this point to evoke the ways in which Kane projects beyond the fictional death, to speculate in various directions as to what 'might have been', even to a certain extent disclaiming authorial responsibility for the death:

> Si le fou ne l'avait pas assassiné, Samba serait resté, et il aurait entrepris là de former, d'ouvrir les gens [...] sur le terrain de l'agronomie, de la technique. S'il avait survécu, il aurait expliqué aux Diallobé qu'on peut être bon musulman, ou pas musulman, tout en étant bon Diallobé. Il leur aurait expliqué qu'on pouvait être musulman sans suivre les tendances les plus extrémistes, les plus exigeantes, des fanatiques, [...] des intégristes. Il aurait pu expliquer cela. C'est ce qu'il aurait fait. Mais il n'a pas eu le temps de le faire, et donc la société n'avait pas encore eu la possibilité de percevoir le message. On lui avait dit d'aller apprendre ailleurs à 'lier le bois au bois', à 'vaincre sans avoir raison', à disposer d'armes et d'outils pour faire progresser la société, et il avait bien appris cela. Mais on ne lui a pas donné le temps d'expliquer ce qu'il avait appris. (*16*)

In terms of an account of Samba Diallo as we see him in the novel, this seems unsatisfactory. There is no evidence at all in the text to suggest that Samba Diallo was professionally prepared to offer technical advice on matters of agronomy etc. to the Diallobé. As we have seen, he is essentially preoccupied by a spiritual and cultural dilemma, and his interests and training are in philosophy rather than anything scientific. In terms of a literary fiction, a writer using autobiographical material has perhaps a greater licence than one creating from nothing to project into the realms of 'what might have been'. But to say that 'on ne lui a pas donné le temps d'expliquer ce qu'il avait appris' side-steps the issue of authorial decision-making. As a solution to this problem, I would suggest that Cheikh Hamidou Kane is projecting beyond his hero's death in two ways. Firstly into the character of Salif Bâ, the main character of his second novel, *Les Gardiens du temple,* trained in France precisely as an agronomist and technical expert, and returned to serve his country in that domain. The author reveals in interview that Salif Bâ, 'c'est un peu un fils de Samba Diallo, un successeur de Samba Diallo, une réincarnation de Samba Diallo' (*14*), although in the text itself Salif Bâ is portrayed meditating on Samba Diallo's death in the following terms:

> Le pays des Diallobe [*sic, passim*] avait été comme foudroyé par cette disparition, car l'homme que le destin avait ravi ainsi n'était pas seulement une personnification presque idéale des valeurs dans lesquelles tous les Diallobe se reconnaissaient, mais, durant le temps qu'il avait vécu parmi les siens, à son retour du pays des Blancs et avant que le Fou ne l'eût sacrifié, il avait aussi commencé d'apparaître aux yeux de ceux qui l'avaient approché comme la preuve incarnée, l'annonciateur d'un avenir fertile. (*2*, p.50)

In this respect one character is both the continuation of the other, and entirely distinct. Salif Bâ has been able to go beyond the contradictions experienced by Samba Diallo, and is able to grasp the future (in the way *la Grande Royale* envisaged, through technical expertise), while bearing witness to his culture of origin (one of the most moving passages in the novel is in the opening pages, where the reader sees Salif Bâ in meditative mood, lying on his back, looking up at the immensity of the starlit sky in the *pays des Diallobé* (*2*, pp.11-12); cf. the unconscious link acknowledged by Kane in *7*, p.6). The time-lapse between the two is also somewhat elastic: in interview with Lise Gauvin, Kane suggests that 'Salif Bâ et tous les héros des *Gardiens du temple* sont des gens qui viennent deux ou trois générations après Samba Diallo...' (*8*, p.145).

The other projection towards the future is, clearly, that of Cheikh Hamidou Kane himself. What Samba Diallo 'would have done', had he been spared, is precisely what the writer himself has done, spending his life in the material development of his country rather than in the ivory tower of philosophical reflection towards which his own inner self was obviously inclined. Samba Diallo's death is thus in some ways a symbolic death of part of Cheikh Hamidou Kane himself, that part of him which was only backward-looking and could not handle the transition to the new. It is only those who, like Cheikh Hamidou Kane himself, or like Salif Bâ, can manage the delicate balancing act between tradition and modernity, that can survive.

There is a third way, however, in which Samba Diallo can be projected, and that is into the past. I have already referred to the way in which the education debate at the centre of *L'Aventure ambiguë* had been part of Diallobé society already for several generations. The generation of Cheikh Hamidou Kane's (great-)grandfather had already had substantial contact with the French school, and had benefited from it. When pressed on this point, the writer conceded that there was in the novel a kind of 'téléscopage du temps', and went on to state that:

> Dans une certaine mesure je crois que Samba Diallo, pour moi, est un peu une sorte de réincarnation et de poursuite de la vie et de l'être de celui qui a été mon arrière-grand-père, Abdoulaye [...]. Je crois que peut-être inconsciemment dans mon esprit, Samba Diallo est une sorte de réincarnation. Abdoulaye est allé jusqu'à ce stade, et à ce moment-là, Samba Diallo est apparu, et a été au-delà. Abdoulaye s'est arrêté à l'Ecole des Otages... (*16*)

Although from the text it would seem that it is *la Grande Royale* who inherited Abdoulaye's temperament and particular pragmatism, rather than the young Samba Diallo, it is nevertheless clear that both characters embody the same values, and that the author's aspirations for his literary double are the same as those characteristics he sees most clearly in his illustrious ancestor. The fact that *la Grande Royale* says of Samba Diallo, 'Pauvre enfant, qui eût dû naître contemporain de ses ancêtres. Je crois qu'il en eût été le guide' (p.133), would seem to bear out Kane's desire to make an implicit link between the contemporary character and Abdoulaye. Samba Diallo would thus be a kind of composite character, a stage through which a certain aspiration for the Diallobé passed, starting with Abdoulaye, continuing briefly in Samba Diallo, before finding literary expression once more in Salif Bâ, with continuity being provided by the real person of the author himself.

What we seem to have, therefore, is a highly individual use on Cheikh Hamidou Kane's part of autobiographical material. The author both is and is not the character he has created, making him a repository for cultural aspirations which continue way beyond the text. He kills this character off, in ambiguous circumstances, but only to resurrect him in further fictional form, and in richer guise. Behind him there is the whole weight of a centuries-old culture, which both Samba Diallo and his creator bear proudly, but which is treated in fictional form with great discretion and discernment in the choice of detail. Everything is distilled, reduced to essentials. If the resulting fiction is sometimes ambiguous, it is a rich and suggestive ambiguity. The central dilemma remains crystal-clear, doubt surrounding only the resolution of that dilemma.

2. Structure, Time and Space

The dilemma at the heart of *L'Aventure ambiguë* is presented as a journey in more ways than one. It is in geographical terms a journey from the *pays des Diallobé* to other parts of an unnamed Senegal, to Paris and finally back to the *pays des Diallobé*. The geographical movement is accompanied, obviously, by a development in time, so that a space-time continuum is created in which the elements, intimately interconnected, are ultimately inseparable. It is also, however, a journey of self-discovery, a type of initiation, rendering the psychological interest of the novel paramount: we are a long way from the *roman d'aventures*, or the picaresque, in which the events themselves dominate. The psychological process borne along by the space-time continuum is thus the major structuring element of the work.

Since the central dilemma experienced by Samba Diallo is brought about by the confrontation between his native culture as he knows it in the *pays des Diallobé* and the Western culture transmitted firstly by the *école étrangère* and then by his experiences in Paris, the novel has a basic polarity of structure, the *pays des Diallobé* being opposed to the technologically driven world of the West. ('West' is, of course, a very inaccurate term, particularly in opposition to the African continent, but it follows Cheikh Hamidou's designation of all that is opposed to traditional society as 'l'Occident' and, as we shall see, the term is a happy linguistic accident in other ways.) This polarity is reflected in the fact that the novel is divided into two parts, of roughly equal length, Part I being set exclusively in Africa, although the West makes incursions already through evocations of the conquest of the *pays des Diallobé* and, more generally, the continent of Africa by the colonising powers, by the dilemma posed by the French school and Samba Diallo's subsequent attendance at it, and by various conversations, including the account by *le fou* of his experiences in Europe. Part II is set mainly in Paris, but there are several scenes which return to the *pays des Diallobé*, as well as

various evocations by the central character of his native land. There is
also Samba Diallo's final, crucial return home, so that as well as the
basic polarity of the novel, there is a tripartite geographical
movement following what might be termed the classic structure of the
récit d'initiation, in which the hero departs from home, learns the
secrets only to be learned elsewhere, and then returns, a different
person, to his native territory, so that, viewed from Samba Diallo's
perspective, the movement is home – 'the West' – home. We shall
return to the relationship between the text and the *récit d'initiation*, as
it is a complex matter. But there is a further tripartite analysis
possible, that based on the dilemma itself, where the movement is
seen in terms of thesis (the *pays des Diallobé*) – antithesis (the West)
– synthesis (the final chapter, or 'epilogue', witnessing to the
impossibility of resolving the dilemma in this life, and therefore
outside time and space).

Within this overall framework the events are presented in a
manner which is not totally sequential, and frequently fragmented.
Sometimes this is due to the use of a flashback technique, which
Moriceau and Rouch divide into genuine flashbacks, where the reader
is taken back in time, though sometimes only to a recent past, and
what they term *souvenirs rapportés*, which are evoked by one or
other of the characters (for example where *le maître* recalls to *la
Grande Royale* the circumstances of her father's death, or *le fou*'s
recollections of Europe) (*28*, p.17). These flashbacks provoke an
effect of fragmentation in the narrative. Thus in chapter 6, which
opens with Samba Diallo walking down the street in L. with his
father, memories of *le maître* provoke a flashback to 'les circon-
stances de son départ du foyer' (p.75), which is then followed by a
scene in which the father receives the letter announcing Samba
Diallo's imminent arrival in L., the Diallobé having decided that he
should attend the *école étrangère*. The chapter closes in a sense
sequentially, after Samba Diallo's arrival, with the *nuit du Coran*, but
it should be noted that in terms of the narrative, this episode precedes
the scene in school which forms the main part of chapter 5, and also
therefore the first part of chapter 6.

Frequently also, the connecting links are missed out between
episodes, and the reader is left to supply them. An example of this is

in the sequence chapter 6 – chapter 7, where we move from the house of *le Chevalier* to the office of Paul Lacroix without any expressed transition. Nor, in general, is the passage of time between one episode and another indicated, although there are exceptions to this, as in the introduction to the scene on the boat, where *le maître* and *le Chevalier* decide that Samba Diallo should attend the Koranic school the following year, and which is noted as happening 'deux ans auparavant' (p.18), or occasional references to 'ce soir-là' (p.34), or 'le lendemain' (p.66). The main effect of this fragmentation is to underline the importance of the psychological aspect of the novel: what is going on in the characters' minds, and notably that of Samba Diallo, is of much greater significance than mere chronology.

In terms of both time and space, at least until Samba Diallo's return to the *pays des Diallobé*, it is clear that the novel follows in general terms Cheikh Hamidou Kane's own itinerary, just as it follows his psychological and spiritual development. An attempt has already been made in chapter 1 to throw some light on the relationship between author and literary creation. But it is important not to try to look for too much precision: Cheikh Hamidou Kane has deliberately left many matters open, in the interests of universalising his subject-matter. It is not necessarily revealing to try and establish an absolute identity of itinerary, as Jean Getrey, for example, has done (*18*, p.21). He wants to make the whole work cover a period of eighteen years, Samba Diallo being six at the beginning and twenty-four at the end. Although the former can be deduced from the text, we know that Cheikh Hamidou Kane was thirty or thirty-one when he returned from Paris in 1958-59. But we also know that Samba Diallo's studies in Paris seem to have been exclusively philosophical, taking presumably less time, and that he may have been called back prematurely by his father (see his letter, pp.175-77). If the author had wanted us to know exactly how long Samba Diallo had remained in Paris, he would presumably have told us. What is important is the transforming process that went on there.

On the question of a deliberate openness in the treatment of time, reference has already been made to what Kane calls 'un téléscopage de temps' between various points in the novel. Questioned in interview on the fact that the *école étrangère* is presented as being a recent arrival in the *pays des Diallobé*, and yet *le Chevalier* has necessarily passed through the system, the author replied 'effectivement [...] il y a comme un téléscopage du temps du récit.' Referring to his perception of Samba Diallo as a reincarnation of his (great)-grandfather Abdoulaye, he added: 'C'est vrai, il y a un téléscopage avec le temps historique, mais un téléscopage aussi entre les générations', and a little later, 'les problèmes évoqués sont des problèmes d'Abdoulaye Kane' (*16*). When asked to pin down *le fou* in terms of the war in which he had apparently fought, he refers to the same phenomenon: 'C'était probablement la première guerre mondiale [...]. Là aussi, il y a un téléscopage entre les deux guerres', adding significantly, 'Ce qu'il faut retenir, c'est que le fou est quelqu'un qui a eu une expérience de l'Occident différente de celle que Samba Diallo a eue.' It is thus the confrontation of the two cultures, provoking a shock from which *le fou* never recovered, which is important, and not the strict historical context.

This 'téléscopage' involves a certain use of anachronism. An interesting use of this phenomenon is in the representation of Demba, whose first act in taking over at *le foyer ardent* as *maître des Diallobé* is to change the Koranic school hours so that pupils might also attend the *école nouvelle*. In fact, he is unlikely to have had recourse to this measure so late in the colonial system: it was made a requirement at the beginning of the century – although not one frequently put into practice – in the attempt by the French to curtail the power of the Koranic schools. Cheikh Hamidou Kane himself, after all, continued to pursue his Koranic studies alongside attendance at the French school. But for Samba Diallo to have to make the abrupt transition from one system to the other is clearly much more dramatic and, in terms of the overall message the author wants to convey, much more effective.

When we consider space in the same light, it is possible to draw the same conclusions. We have already noted the deliberate lack of geographical precision throughout the text in respect of Senegal. In Paris, we have references to 'le Boulevard Saint-Michel', which serves to designate more generally the *quartier latin*, various cafés, the metro (but which?), and a pleasure-boat, presumably in the Bois de Boulogne or somewhere similar. Compare the information we have on Paris in *L'Aventure ambiguë* with the information James Joyce supplies on Dublin in *Ulysses*. Whereas a reader could find his way around Dublin from Joyce's remarkably precise evocations, it would be a singularly disadvantaged traveller who had to find his way around Paris on our narrator's instructions! But Paris is a symbol, the place of exile, where the distance, both geographical and spiritual, from the *pays des Diallobé* is felt most acutely.

It can even be a disadvantage to read into the text geographical precision which is not supplied: for instance, in the episode where *le maître* offers the fine thoroughbred he has been given by the *Chef des Diallobé* to the *Directeur de l'école nouvelle*. Because the reader has no idea of the geography involved, the account is accepted quite naturally as part of the narrative. In fact, when one knows the identity of L., the problem of transporting the animal some four hundred kilometres becomes acute. A horse-box would not have been an option in the *pays des Diallobé*. If the episode ever took place, the likelihood is that the horse was taken the hundred yards up the sandy track from Thierno's house to the *Directeur de l'école étrangère* in Saldé. The reader is also unlikely to know that such a school already existed in Saldé: the young Kane was presumably sent to Louga rather than there in order that *la Grande Royale* could get him as far away from Thierno as possible. Too much precision in such a case is indeed a hindrance.

So far we have considered space and time mainly in everyday terms, although we have already indicated ways in which chronological sequence is sometimes disrupted. But Cheikh Hamidou Kane introduces in both respects another dimension. When relating to time, this manifests itself as an irruption into the horizontal, linear, historical development of the narrative of a vertical dimension relating to the spiritual development of one or other of the characters. It refers to sudden flashes of inspiration, a sudden illumination, or to moments of prayer interspersed in the narrative. (Note, of course, that prayer is one of the five 'pillars' of Islam, and that the Muslim day is broken up by times of prayer regarded as an obligation by every true believer.) These brief moments of respite in the onward movement of the narrative are of singular importance in the development of the main action, that is to say, the unfolding of the spiritual destiny of Samba Diallo and certain other characters.

One such moment occurs when Samba Diallo is with Jean Lacroix, on the path leading from his father's office. As the sun begins to set, Samba Diallo breaks off the conversation in order to pray:

> Samba Diallo se leva, se tourna vers l'Est, leva les bras, mains ouvertes, et les laissa tomber, lentement. Sa voix retentit. Jean n'osa pas contourner son camarade pour observer son visage, mais il lui sembla que cette voix n'était plus la sienne. Il restait immobile. Rien ne vivait en lui, que cette voix qui parlait au crépuscule une langue que Jean ne comprenait pas. Puis son long caftan blanc que le soir teintait de violet fut parcouru d'un frisson. Le frisson s'accentua en même temps que la voix montait. Le frisson devint un frémissement qui secoua le corps tout entier et la voix, un sanglot. A l'Est, le ciel était un immense cristal couleur de lilas. (pp.71-72)

Samba Diallo here is transformed, reduced to a voice which is no longer his. The sunset, 'cette mort pathétique et belle du jour' (p.72), introduces a cosmic element into the whole episode, reinforced doubtless by the abrupt contrast between the immense skies and the flat, largely featureless landscapes of Senegal. In this scene, while contemplating his friend, Jean loses all sense of time, and is only roused from the spectacle by the arrival of Samba Diallo's father, at which the forward movement of the narrative again picks up.

Another significant illustration of the same phenomenon occurs during the episode known as *la nuit du Coran*, when Samba Diallo, arriving at L., having finished his Koranic studies, devotes the first night to the recitation from memory of the whole of the Koran for his parents. Again, cosmic elements are present: the scene is set with the remark: 'le lumineux crépuscule s'était à peine éteint qu'au ciel un millier d'étoiles avait germé. La lune naquit au cœur de leur festival scintillant et la nuit, subitement, parut s'emplir d'une exaltation mystique' (p.83).[2] As *le Chevalier* listens to his son, he seems to experience the same suspension of the normal laws of nature that *le maître des Diallobé* had experienced on listening to his pupil, a feeling transmitted to him by the trance-like state of Samba Diallo himself:

> Sa voix à peine audible d'abord s'affermit et s'éleva par gradation. Progressivement, il sentit que l'envahissait un sentiment comme il n'en avait jamais éprouvé auparavant. [...] Le chevalier [...] s'était dressé à la voix de Samba Diallo et il semblait maintenant qu'en entendant la Parole il subît la même lévitation qui exhaussait le maître. (pp.83-84)

Martin Lings, in his introduction to Sufi doctrine, gives an interesting commentary on the significance for Sufism of the recitation of the Koran, which could be applied here. He sees such a recitation as a way of experiencing *fanâ'*, extinction of the created element in the uncreated:

> The Sufis speak of 'seeking to be drowned' (*istighrâq*) in the verses of the Qur'ân which are, according to one of the most fundamental doctrines of Islam, the Uncreated Word of God. What they are seeking is, to use another Sufi term, extinction (*fanâ*) of the created in the Uncreated, of the temporal in the Eternal, of the finite in

---

[2] One is reminded here of a passage from the 'récit initiatique peul' known as *L'Eclat de la grande étoile*, which Cheikh Hamidou Kane would certainly have known, where the young Tiôlel contemplates the starry sky:
'Tiôlel était là, debout, en train d'observer. / Son regard se hissait au ciel. / Ce qui inquiète tout le monde ne l'inquiète pas. / Les étoiles rayent les étapes de l'espace qu'il regarde; / des lueurs les suivent, semblables à des queues. / Les étoiles enchantent Tiôlel au point de le fasciner. / Elles brillent dans le ciel, tels des yeux / de chat d'un éclat pur, étincelant; / elles ornent l'empyrée; quelle nuit splendide! / une nuit mirée du fourreau de son éternité!' (*43*, p. 27)

the Infinite; and for some Sufis the recitation of the Qur'an has been, throughout life, their chief means of concentration upon God which is itself the essence of every spiritual path. (*59*, p.25)

A previous vision of *le Chevalier*'s, less happy this time, occurs just before the *nuit du Coran*, and is provoked by the bitter reflection that the decision to send his son to the *école étrangère* has ensured a second victory of the colonisers over his people, whose idolatry will lead to a complete loss of identity:

A ce moment de ses réflexions, le chevalier eut comme une vision hallucinée. Un point de notre globe brillait d'un éclat aveuglant, comme si un foyer immense y eût été allumé. Au cœur de ce brasier, un grouillement d'humains semblait se livrer à une incompréhensible et fantastique mimique d'adoration. Débouchant de partout, de profondes vallées d'ombres déversaient des flots d'êtres humains de toutes les couleurs, d'êtres qui, à mesure qu'ils approchaient du foyer, épousaient insensiblement le rythme ambiant et, sous l'effet de la lumière, perdaient leurs couleurs originales pour la blafarde teinte qui recouvrait tout alentour. (p.82)

Finally, mention should be made of the epilogue to the novel, where Samba Diallo in death leaves the space-time continuum definitively. We shall return to the complexities of this final chapter later, but for the moment suffice it to say that it seems to represent the realisation for all eternity of the partial vision which has been accorded Samba Diallo throughout his quest.

The question of moments 'outside time' leads us to the consideration of a fundamental difference in attitude between an African, more specifically a Muslim, and a 'Western' concept of time, as epitomised in *L'Aventure ambiguë*. Regarding the past, it is a commonplace since Hegel, however wrongheaded, to say that 'Africans have no history'. The narrator makes ironic reference to this widely held misapprehension in the flashback account of the conquest of the *pays des Diallobé* when he says, 'Ceux qui n'avaient point d'histoire rencontraient ceux qui portaient le monde sur leurs épaules [...]. Ils étaient sans passé, donc sans souvenir' (p.59). The passage itself gives a lie to this view, since it is the record, passed on orally but none the less living, of a traumatic event in the life of the community. Samba Diallo himself is clearly steeped in a consciousness of his roots, which he knows in minute detail: his vocation is essentially to fulfil himself as a Diallobé. It is a different attitude to the past from the written records on which Western historians have traditionally worked, but it is probably true to say that the past conditions the present of Africans far more than it does that of the average European. To know the past is vital to decide what action to take in the present. Dominique Zahan underlines the 'regressive' nature of African reasoning: 'je fais ceci parce que mes pères l'ont fait. Et eux l'ont fait parce que notre ancêtre l'a fait' (*77*, p.79). The ideal is therefore a constant repetition of the past, enriched each time by the present moment, 'un ensemble de valeurs rapportées au passé' (*77*, p.86; see also *61*, p.17).

What is true of African society in general is true in this instance of Islam in Africa: if you want to know what to do today, look backwards. Hence the incapacity of *le maître* to tell his community how to act in respect of *l'école nouvelle*. His world by definition cannot change. Allah has communicated his last word through his prophet Muhammed, and there is no room for incorporating a Western-style world. As he says to *la Grande Royale*, 'Madame, Dieu a clos la sublime lignée de ses envoyés avec notre prophète Mohammed, la bénédiction soit sur lui. Le dernier messager nous a transmis l'ultime Parole où tout a été dit. Seuls les insensés attendent encore' (p.46). The dilemma of *le maître* is thus more radical than a simple inability to make up his mind. Those who, like *la Grande Royale*, see the necessity of moving forward, recommend it as a course of action with a heavy heart: they know that change is inevitable, that Diallobé society will never be the same again, even if they manage to save certain key values of that society. The world of *le maître* cannot incorporate such change.

The difference discernible between the Western attitude to the past and that of Islam is noticeable also in respect of the future. An excellent illustration of this dichotomy is to be found in the conversation between Paul Lacroix and *le Chevalier*. Faced with *le Chevalier*, the epitome of traditional aristocracy, Lacroix meditates on the African unwillingness to work for what they do not have:

> La vérité qu'ils n'ont pas maintenant, qu'ils sont incapables de conquérir, ils l'espèrent pour la fin. Ainsi, pour la justice aussi. Tout ce qu'ils veulent et qu'ils n'ont pas, au lieu de chercher à le conquérir, ils l'attendent à la fin. [...] Quant à nous, chaque jour, nous conquérons un peu plus de vérité, grâce à la science. (p.88)

Samba Diallo's Marxist friend, Lucienne, has inevitably the same proactive attitude as Lacroix: instead of waiting passively for the will of God to be accomplished, she chooses action to right the ills of the world, and to make things happen (see pp.128-29 and 153-55).

The discussion between Lacroix and *le Chevalier* begins with their divergence in view on 'the end of the world'. Here there is a distinction to be made also between a traditional African way of looking at this aspect of the future, and the Muslim. For traditional Africa, there is no 'end of the world': it will continue just as long as there are ancestors to sustain it, and they will be there as long as there is new human life to continue the chain of being. Hence the importance of procreation. The Muslim attitude, which is represented here by *le Chevalier*, is quite different: the end of the world has a teleological quality, it is a metaphysical, transcendent entity bound up with man's spiritual destiny. 'Notre monde est celui qui croit à la fin du monde', he says. 'Qui l'espère et la craint tout à la fois' (p.89). They fear it because it is also the day of Judgement, when the acts of each person will be assessed and their fate determined. This is made clear in the Koran, in *Suras* LXIX and LXX, for example. In the meantime, the faithful have only to follow God's commandments, laid down once and for all and communicated by the Prophet. The future is thus seen as conformity with the pre-ordained will of God, rather than goal-orientated.

Lacroix's Western vision is different again. Rejecting *le Chevalier*'s cosmic vision, he will accept only the kind of end to the world that science can explain, a cataclysmic event on a physical plane that would destroy the planet. In the meantime, man's task through science is to uncover every day a little more truth. *Le Chevalier* rejects this: for him, partial truth is of no fundamental significance: what is important is Truth, which will be revealed at the end of the world. He muses silently to himself: 'Ils ne voient pas que la vérité qu'ils découvrent chaque jour est chaque jour plus étriquée. Un peu de vérité chaque jour... bien sûr, il le faut, c'est nécessaire. Mais la Vérité?' (p.89).

It is these attitudes and beliefs of a Muslim society that *le pays des Diallobé* is made to incarnate. For Kane, the traditional African world is the world of Muslim Africa, and Islam is the most 'natural' religion for Africans: as he writes, 'Si l'Islam n'est pas la seule religion de l'Afrique occidentale, elle en est la première par l'importance. Je veux dire aussi qu'il me semble qu'elle est la religion de son cœur' (pp.6-7). (The writer has in fact been reproached for seemingly forgetting that Islam is not native to West Africa, being a 'foreign' import.) There is thus total identity between the spirit of Islam and the spirit of the *pays des Diallobé*, and even though the latter can be identified geographically on a map, it is, as Moriceau and Rouch say, '[un] pays dont l'étendue *intérieure* semble dépasser la réalité géographique' (*20*, p.14). Mouralis speaks of the evocation in the African novel of '[le] déchirement de l'individu arraché malgré lui à ce temps mythique de la tribu et hors duquel la vie semble n'avoir aucun goût' (*64*, p.81). The *pays des Diallobé* is, spatially, the place from which Samba Diallo is progressively exiled, a true paradise lost. It is his spiritual centre, and this fact is expressed in a number of images relating to the centre and the periphery. In Paris, Samba Diallo confesses to Adèle: 'Je ne brûle plus au cœur des êtres et des choses' (p.174). *Les Blancs* responsible for his Western education have transformed him: 'Progressivement, ils me firent émerger du cœur des choses et m'habituèrent à prendre mes distances du monde' (p.173). Pierre-Louis's engineer son, Marc, makes the same point when he refers to 'notre vigueur qui nous place d'emblée au cœur intime de la chose' (p.164). In his conversation with Paul

Lacroix, *le Chevalier* talks of 'une vérité profonde', and contrasts it with 'l'évidence [qui] est une qualité de surface. Votre science', he says to Lacroix, 'est le triomphe de l'évidence, une prolifération de la surface. Elle fait de vous les maîtres de l'extérieur mais en même temps elle vous y exile, de plus en plus' (p.90). There seems to be an echo here, conscious or unconscious, of Leo Frobenius when, referring to the progress made in the sciences in the nineteenth century, the celebrated ethnologist writes: 'Par un travail forcené [l'humanité] acquérait une vision générale de la surface, mais non une vue intuitive en profondeur. Elle n'aboutissait qu'à une reproduction extrêmement fine, en miniature, de la surface du monde' (*52*, p.11). Hence the mania for the collection of objects, for accumulation, which characterised the eighteenth and particularly the nineteenth centuries, and which resulted in the great museums of the Western world. 'Knowing' the world, in popular perception at least, was reduced to possessing specimens of its diversity. 'Mais la vue d'ensemble des phénomènes et la pénétration à travers les faits jusqu'à la réalité intérieure restaient inaccessibles à l'humanité'. Senghor's distinction between *objective* and *subjective* knowledge is founded on the same perception; the exterior reality of things is made up of signs, whose significance is an entry into Being itself (*69*, p.73).

The contrasting world-views are given a different spatial expression in this same dialogue when *le Chevalier* refers to the world of Lacroix as 'un monde rond et parfait' (p.88). Lacroix has undermined traditional cosmology in the following words: 'Malheureusement, pour nous, c'est mon univers qui est vrai. La terre n'est pas plate. Elle n'a pas de versants qui donnent sur l'abîme. Le soleil n'est pas un lampadaire fixé sur un dais de porcelaine bleue'. There is no reason to believe, of course, that *le Chevalier*, a sophisticated individual who has in any case studied Western science and philosophy, imagines this world-view to be literally true. But it is nevertheless necessary to his sense of man's destiny, as is demonstrated at the end of the dialogue, where he outlines to Lacroix what he sees to be traditional society's contribution to 'la cité future' in terms of 'l'abîme', 'l'ombre', the mystery of the universe which is denied by science because it thinks it has abolished the need for it:

Je sais que vous ne croyez pas en l'ombre. Ni à la fin. Ce
que vous ne voyez pas n'est pas. L'instant, comme un
radeau, vous transporte sur la face lumineuse de son
disque rond, et vous niez tout l'abîme qui vous entoure.
La cité future, grâce à mon fils, ouvrira ses baies sur
l'abîme, d'où viendront de grandes bouffées d'ombre sur
nos corps desséchés, sur nos fronts altérés. (p.92)

These images, combining both space and time, owe their
effectiveness to a certain paradoxical quality. It is man's
uncertainties, his ignorance in the face of his final destiny, his
'angoisse', which are given as desirable, whereas the light of
knowledge and Western science is portrayed as limited and therefore
ultimately treacherous.

Le Chevalier is able to compare the two world-views because
he has had a certain experience of Western civilisation to set
alongside the more intimate knowledge he has of his own. His son
will go down the same path but, we are led to believe, will cover an
even greater distance by the continuation of his studies in Paris. The
ability to see one's own society from the outside, and the learning
process which this implies, involves inevitably a certain loss of
innocence: Adam and Eve did not know they were naked until
Paradise was effectively lost, just as Samba Diallo in the *pays des
Diallobé* is in a state of undifferentiated innocence which is broken
only by his exposure to Western values. To what extent can the
learning process in which he is involved be associated with traditional
accounts of initiation? Can *L'Aventure ambiguë* be read as a modern
récit d'initiation? African writing in French of this general period
contains many descriptions of initiation rites, intended either to
convey to the European reader the essential of African civilisation, as
in Laye Camara's *L'Enfant noir*, or to criticise traditional customs for
their injustice, which is rather the point of view of Ahmadou
Kourouma in *Les Soleils des indépendances*. Perhaps even more
relevant for our purposes are the Fulbe initiation texts, such as
Koumen and *Kaïdara*, which are very much part of Cheikh Hamidou
Kane's cultural heritage, and whose influence he freely recognises
(*16*). These are long oral poems, recited over generations by the

pastoral nomadic Fulbe, as part of the initiation rites of the young herdsman, who learned progressively the secrets of the pastoral life, allowing him to be 'reborn' into a new life, where practical knowledge regarding the care of cattle is combined with a mystical union with the deity who protects them and the whole of the community. The knowledge imparted thus goes way beyond mere husbandry. Germaine Dieterlen, in the notes to the edition of *Koumen* which she prepared with Amadou Hampâté Bâ, makes the following comment:

> L'initiation est connaissance: connaissance de Dieu et des règles qu'il a instaurées, connaissance de soi, aussi, car elle se présente comme une éthique; connaissance également de tout ce qui n'est pas l'homme, 'puisqu'il lui a été donné de connaître ce qui n'est pas lui.' Et cette science doit atteindre l'universel, chacun de ses éléments et de ses aspects faisant partie d'un tout; les Peuls disaient 'Tout ne se sait pas. Tout ce qu'on sait, c'est une partie du tout.' (*42*, p. 93; see also *40* and *38*, pp.151-61)

Cheikh Hamidou Kane has stated that the learning process which goes on in the *foyer ardent* is in fact a process of initiation: 'Il n'y a pas d'éducation qui se fasse sans souffrance. [...] On met à l'épreuve soi-même, son identité. C'est ce que Samba Diallo a compris de l'enseignement du maître des Diallobé' (*15*). Thus the account of the educative process at the *foyer ardent* bears many of the characteristics of initiation, requiring the ability to bear suffering, the submission of the individual will to a higher cause, in this case the child's spiritual destiny, total obedience to the initiation-master (here the *maître des Diallobé*), who imparts knowledge which is revealed only partially, as the various stages in the initiation process are completed. It is also an education, unlike that of the *école étrangère*, which addresses the whole person, not just the intellect (*16*). But Samba Diallo has to leave the *foyer ardent* at a critical stage, before his initiation is complete; on the other hand, the learning process goes on throughout the journey to Europe and back. Is it possible to see in the continuation of Samba Diallo's 'ambiguous adventure' a genuine initiation process? Can one call it, as Jeanne-Lydie Goré does, '[la] transposition sur un plan intellectuel du Graal Noir' (*28*, p.73)? William Calin likewise believes that Cheikh Hamidou Kane reproduces universal literary archetypes through the introduction of the vocabulary and imagery of quest-romance into his novel (*22*, p. 187).

From the point of view of Diallobé society, the path traced out for Samba Diallo is certainly a quest. On parting with her cousin, *la Grande Royale* tells him: 'Va savoir chez eux comment l'on peut vaincre sans avoir raison' (p.165), in other words, he is to find out the conquerors' secrets, which are vital to the physical survival of the Diallobé. And indeed, he is successful in his mission, he learns those secrets – hence his distress at becoming a hybrid being (p.125). On Samba Diallo's part, the thirst for knowledge, always a necessary part of an initiation process, is certainly there: he is seduced from the beginning by the white man's language, and the entry it gives him into a new world (see pp.172-73). It also involves him in suffering and hardship, and the apprenticeship of self-discipline. But whereas in the traditional initiation process, the postulant has a guide throughout, Samba Diallo progressively loses his guides. He is cut off from *maître Thierno* from the moment he leaves the *pays des Diallobé*, and although his father accompanies him a little further on the way, he has no one by the time he arrives in Paris, and is increasingly isolated. And whereas, for example, the postulant Silé in *Koumen* receives succour from Foroforondou, the wife of Koumen, at one and the same time Woman, Initiator and Mother, Samba Diallo is bereft of genuine female support. He rediscovers the life-support of '[le] lait maternel' only after death (p.190), having rejected the Mother-figure for God, the male principle. As he says to Lucienne, 'Je crois que je préfère Dieu à ma mère' (p.156; see *22*, p.194).

It is surely significant, furthermore, that through a number of interesting coincidences of language, he is going 'in the wrong direction' to gain genuine wisdom. The people of the Futa Toro have always migrated, mainly for economic reasons. There is in fact a Pular saying, *So mi mayani, mi yahate hirnangué*, 'If I don't die, I will go to the West', since the West is inevitably the direction in which all the big cities lie in relation to the Futa (*74*, p. 21). The West is therefore associated with economic prosperity and individual adventure, but cultural exile as far as the *Hal-pulaar'en* are concerned. There is in addition the myth of exile on which the culture of the nomadic Fulbe is founded; they see themselves as originating in the East, and bound therefore to return (*43*, p.51, n.1). The association of exile with the West, and with the East as spiritual home, is a constant in the mystical and Sufi tradition of Islam: Henri Corbin, in his study of Avicenna, refers to the *Récit de Havy ibn Yaqzân*, and his perception of 'l'orient' as the place of spiritual fulfilment, rather than anywhere that can be identified on a map. One is spiritually, rather than geographically 'orientated'. Likewise, 'l'Occident' is the non-geographical location where the soul feels itself to be a spiritual stranger (*49*, pp.17-18.) In the same context, Corbin mentions the writings of Sohrawardi, and the 'exil occidental de l'âme' evoked by Cheikh Hamidou Kane himself in the address published in *Esprit* (*3*, pp.378-79). As to being influenced by these writings, or by those of other Sufi mystics, when writing *L'Aventure ambiguë*, he stated in interview that he probably knew of some of them at that time, but that the main influence was through 'l'ambiance dans laquelle j'ai baigné dans ma famille', especially that generated by his paternal grandfather, already mentioned, the Qaadi of Matam (*16*). The fact that Dominique Zahan writes of a 'valorisation de l'espace sur l'axe est-ouest' in African philosophy by and large, whereby the East is identified with life, health, well-being generally, and the West with sickness, ill-luck and death, only serves to emphasise what seems to be a general spiritual climate, a whole traditional world, whose influence on his development Kane would be the first to recognise (*77*, p.107). The continuous spiritual presence of the East is of course reinforced in the text by the numerous references to turning to the East to pray.

Samba Diallo's 'aventure occidentale' would seem therefore to be a mirror-image of the true initiation quest. His purpose in 'going West' is to seek out the secrets of science and technology which will promote the physical survival of his people (one thinks of the injunction to 'go West, young man'), and the West with which he comes into contact (that represented by thinking from Descartes onwards, at least), is preoccupied with material well-being and the surface of things, rather than their spiritual being. That being so, the quest could succeed only on the material plane, and the initiation was bound to be the opposite of that represented by the *foyer ardent*. It is none the less a journey into the self in which a learning process takes place, a journey which is both geographically and metaphorically 'into the West', but which is ultimately 'not so much in time and space, but within the spirit of the quester' (*38*, p.145).

3. Word and Image

Even a cursory reading of *L'Aventure ambiguë* reveals a very particular preoccupation with language, an effort to 'write well' in the sense of an appeal to the most classical devices of the French language. As in the great French Classical writers, there is a deliberate spareness, a condensation of language, defined by Jean Getrey as 'l'art de suggérer le maximum d'idées à travers le minimum de mots', while he notes the 'expression profondément originale' of the text, 'qui semble unique dans la littérature francophone' (*18*, pp.64, 63). Jeanne-Lydie Goré writes of 'son lyrisme [...] discret, hautain, sans rien de la nostalgie païenne ou de l'exubérance des grands chants venus du continent noir et des îles. L'Afrique elle-même n'est point ici présence chaude et magique. L'accent du récit est limpide, presque abstrait' (*28*, p.73). Hubert de Leusse speaks of its 'austérité voulue' (*58*, p.215), while some critics have interpreted this as a lack of defining colour. Thus P.-H. Simon criticises the language of the novel as being 'parfois trop dissertant, et trop bien écrit, car tout le monde, même *la Grande Royale* y parle un langage de congrès de philosophes' (*36*, p.123). Cheikh Hamidou Kane has defended himself on this charge, by turning what seems to be an accusation into a positive virtue. Expressing his concern for a 'maîtrise de la langue qu'on utilise', he continues: 'Je crois dans la nécessité de s'efforcer de maîtriser l'outil qu'on emploie. Lorsqu'on prétend écrire en français ou en portugais, qu'on n'écrive donc pas du petit nègre sous prétexte qu'on est Nègre' (*5*, p.10). In interview with Lise Gauvin, he reiterates, 'Pour pouvoir écrire, et écrire en français ou en anglais, il faut s'astreindre à une discipline. Je ne suis pas de ceux qui pensent qu'on peut être un bon écrivain en ne maîtrisant pas la langue qu'on utilise' (*8*, p.141). In the same interview, when asked to explain the motivation for the 'français très classique, très châtié, [...] un français presque de puriste' used in *L'Aventure ambiguë*, he replied:

C'est peut-être la marque que les écrivains classiques que je lisais ont laissée en moi. C'est aussi une espèce de tribut que je dois rendre aux gens qui m'ont enseigné cette langue, mes instituteurs sénégalais et français ainsi que les professeurs. Je crois que c'est la conjonction de ces deux faits: principalement la lecture des auteurs classiques, philosophes comme romanciers, qui a imprimé sa marque; et d'autre part, les enseignants, les maîtres. (*8*, p.149)

But can the sober elegance of language of *L'Aventure ambiguë* be reduced to the combined forces of a desire to emulate the great Classical French writers, and to pay a debt of gratitude to his former teachers? It does not seem likely. Here one must recall that Kane's native culture is not French; as we have already seen, one of his main aims in composing his novel was to bear witness to the traditional society in which he had grown up. It is a tradition which has two different but interwoven strands, the oral culture of Fulbe society on the one hand, and the Islamic culture which so influenced Kane's earliest years, through his family and then through the Koranic school.

Scholars are agreed on the great importance of the spoken word to Fulbe society. The very fact that the Tokolor prefer to define themselves by their language, as *Hal-pulaar'en*, is significant. In a lecture given at the first *Congrès International des Ecrivains et Artistes Noirs* in Paris in 1956, Amadou Hampâté Bâ maintains that: 'La plus haute manifestation du génie peul est sans aucun doute son parler', a fact all the more remarkable in that this rich and supple language 'est due à un peuple analphabète vivant dispersé sur des étendues considérables, en pleine brousse, parmi le bétail et non loin des fauves' (*39*, p.88). Hampâté Bâ suggests what might be a reason for this prodigious development among a nomadic people, when he notes a little later in the same lecture: 'La culture peule est purement intellectuelle. Le matériel entrait peu dans les besoins de cette race. Il n'y entre pas encore tout à fait malgré la richesse considérable que constitue le cheptel dont elle est maîtresse' (*ibid.*, p.96). To a people constantly on the move, material possessions would be a hindrance rather than a sign of cultural wealth. The word on the other hand is infinitely transportable. The intellectual nature of Fulbe culture is again helpful in understanding the defining characteristics of *L'Aventure ambiguë*, its lack of 'materiality', local colour and superfluous detail.

It is clear, however, that the importance of the word in oral societies generally is not simply a question of filling a void: when the survival of a whole tradition depends on the way in which things are conveyed orally, when history is handed down through the spoken word, then the art of saying things *well* and therefore memorably becomes immensely important. Does this not have a bearing on Cheikh Hamidou Kane's approach to writing in French? Geneviève Calame-Griaule underlines the importance accorded in oral African discourse to correctness of speech, to nuance, to elegance of expression. The person who 'speaks well' is admired and valued, and at all levels of society mastery of language is a source of prestige and social status. The art of the *griot* is only a particularly accomplished example of a widespread African phenomenon (*45*, pp.74-75). The Fulbe in particular favour an *indirect* way of expressing important truths, proceeding by allusion, enigma and proverb, so that one can say difficult or dangerous things without appearing to do so (*45*, p.83). It is a form of politeness, of respect for the other, that is no doubt essential for everyday relationships in a closed and self-contained society.

On another level the word is at the centre of the religious life of the Fulbe, creating and sustaining the cosmic sense of their universe. According to Ibrahima Sow, it is at the heart of the initiation rites which are the material of so much of their poetry. In this sense, the word is a great deal more than a mere utterance, as he explains in the following passage:

> L'initiation commence avec l'apprentissage de la parole et s'achève avec la maîtrise de la parole. [...] La parole est force. Elle est au commencement et à la fin; et toute l'initiation est en somme un voyage au cours duquel le postulant en apprenant à mieux nommer apprend à mieux parler, à parler juste comme le fait le poète lequel en

parlant, instaure le monde à chaque fois en s'y produisant
lui-même chaque fois. (*71*, p.68)

Examples of the power of the word in African society could be
multiplied. Thus for the Dogon people, *Nommo* is the vital force of
the creator-God Amma, at one and the same time water, fire, blood
and sperm, the creative Word without which nothing on earth is
activated into life. On a practical level, this means that it is not
sufficient for the farmer to sow seed; for it to develop he must
pronounce words that alone have the capacity to bring it to new life
(see *55*, pp.116, 139). The Word is thus creative of Being, rather than
being simply the light of Reason as in the European tradition. It is
non-rational, creating rather than revealing meaning or elaborating an
argument. This rather absolute distinction between African and
European perceptions does not take into account, of course, a whole
Western tradition of poetics, which attributes in the same way a
mystical, creative role to the Word.

It is clear therefore both that in traditional African culture in
general the creation and transmission of meaning is dependent on the
word, and that this word is more powerful and more all-embracing
than is customarily the case in Western society. Recalling the society
in which he grew up, and the importance of the oral dimension on
him as a writer, Kane declared:

> Le medium unique, ou dominant, dans cette culture orale,
> c'est la parole. [...] Tous les échanges se font par la
> parole, les plus fondamentaux, en tout cas. C'est cela qui
> reflète l'importance de la parole. Et quand j'ai appris à
> lire et à écrire, je crois que mon style, le style de mon
> écriture, est façonné par la maîtrise que j'ai de ma langue
> maternelle, le pulaar. (*16*)

More specifically, he recognises the influence of the Pular
récits initiatiques, *Koumen*, *Kaïdara*, etc., in the development of his
style in French: 'Quelque part', he says, 'ces récits initiatiques ont
façonné ma manière d'écrire' (*ibid.*; see also *14*). The influence was
unconscious at first, but re-reading both *L'Aventure ambiguë* and *Les*

Gardiens du temple, he realises that those passages which give him the greatest satisfaction are those in which he can discern the oral tradition of the *récits initiatiques* (*16*). *L'Aventure ambiguë* he characterises as 'très pulaar' (*12*) in its writing. To see from another perspective the relationship Kane creates between his native language and the French in which he conveyed the experiences of his formative years, it is interesting to note that *L'Aventure ambiguë* was translated into Pular in 1990 by a relative of Kane's, Abuubakri Dem. In an interview with Jane Alison Hale, Dem made various comments regarding the translation (*29*, p.9). Asked whether he thought Kane had composed the book mentally in French or in Pular, he replied 'without hesitation': 'French. Obviously, he had a basic social upbringing underlying his thoughts, but as a philosopher he was obliged to write all the rhetoric, all the discussions with politicians [*sic*], scholars, etc. [in French]'. The most difficult passages to translate were apparently those dealing with the materialistic ideas of the *école étrangère*, 'those ideas for which there was no system of reference in Pular', whereas the easiest, according to Dem, were those touching on religion, since, as he said, 'everything that can be thought in human terms finds expression in Pular. But when one comes to political discourse, Communism, it's another type of speech.' Leaving aside the ambiguity of meaning of 'everything that can be thought in human terms' if it does not include 'political discourse' etc., it is in fact possible to see what he means: there is a marked stylistic difference between the passages of mystical exaltation and the philosophical discussions, framed in the mode of Samba Diallo's Western schooling, a difference to which we will return.

The intuition of the novelist and critic Boubacar Boris Diop would seem to be borne out by these reflections on the influence of Kane's native tongue on his writing in French, when he finds himself wondering, in his review of *Les Gardiens du temple*:

> si cette expression racée et sévère n'a pas davantage à voir avec les mouvements à la fois amples et retenus, si caractéristiques de la gestuelle pulaar, qu'avec un académisme crispé. Kourouma avait déporté le parler

malinké dans la langue française, Cheikh Hamidou Kane
y fait entrer les longues périodes du parler pulaar.
(24, p.204)

The evocation of Kourouma is interesting: with Kane, one
could not be further from the re-invention of the French language
which is Kourouma's enterprise. Whereas *Les Soleils des
indépendances* aims to transpose directly into French the popular
speech of Malinké, it seems that what is meant by 'les longues
périodes du parler pulaar' is the stylised, hieratic language of Fulbe
poetry. It is the *virtues* of stylisation, the hieratic *quality* of the
language which pass into French, rather than an attempt to *translate*
in any direct sense.

It is clearly impossible to make a categorical statement
regarding the importance of Cheikh Hamidou Kane's native language
on his writing in French without an intimate knowledge of Pular. But
there seems to be much evidence, in terms both of the general
importance of the spoken word among the Fulbe, and of Kane's own
convictions on the matter, to deduce a substantial influence. The
evidence would seem to justify totally in any case a consideration of
elements outside the French language.

There is, however, another element to consider, to which we
have already alluded, and that is the influence of Muslim culture on
Kane's writing. Islam is, after all, the religion of the Word, handed
down by Allah to the Prophet himself, and as such definitive,
unchanging and unchangeable. Hence the uncontrollable anger of
maître Thierno when Samba Diallo stumbles over a detail in his
repetition of the Koran: 'Ces paroles, le Maître du Monde les a
véritablement prononcées. Et toi, misérable moisissure de la terre,
quand tu as l'honneur de les répéter après lui, tu te négliges au point
de les profaner' (p.14). The Word is supreme knowledge, supreme
illumination (see *21* for a semiotic study of the Word in *L'Aventure
ambiguë*). For Sufis, the recitation of the Koran, the 'uncreated Word
of God', is the essential act on the long road back to the Divine. The
historical accident which has meant that the majority of Muslims in
sub-Saharan Africa recite the Koran in Arabic without understanding
its literal meaning, does not in any way devalue the practice: Kane

conveys clearly the mystical charge of this recitation in his account of Samba Diallo's *nuit du Coran*, an incantation representing a timeless moment in which the boy takes his place in the long tradition of his ancestors. Martin Lings underlines the validity of such a recitation by people who do not understand Arabic, when he writes: 'Their minds are penetrated by the consciousness that they are partaking of the Divine Word. [...] Moreover they are conscious that the Qur'ân is a flow and an ebb – that it flows to them from God and that its verses are miraculous signs (*âyât*) which will take them back to God, and that is precisely why they read it' (*59*, pp.25-26).

The account of the *nuit du Coran* given by Kane in *L'Aventure ambiguë* is perhaps a good place to start a more detailed analysis of the workings of language in the text. It is also instructive to compare it with a passage celebrating a similar event, in Abdoulaye Elimane Kane's novel *La Maison au figuier*, also set (though again without naming it) in Saldé. In *L'Aventure ambiguë*, the scene is both austere and emotionally highly charged. 'Le lumineux crépuscule' is followed by 'un millier d'étoiles [...]. La lune naquit au cœur de leur festival scintillant et la nuit, subitement, parut s'emplir d'une exaltation mystique' (p.83*)*. While making Samba Diallo part of a long ancestral tradition, it is also a moment of intense personal significance for the boy: he knows he is marking the end of an age, and the stars participate in this ending: 'Ce scintillement d'étoiles au-dessus de sa tête, n'était-il pas le verrou constellé rabattu sur une époque révolue? Derrière le verrou, un monde de lumière stellaire brillait doucement, qu'il importait de glorifier une dernière fois' (p.84). The cold brilliance of the stars is full of mystical intensity, while the ghosts of Samba Diallo's ancestors mingle death inextricably with life. His voice becomes that of the 'fantômes aphones' that he has evoked, and the passage ends with Samba Diallo spanning both past and future, with him mourning his ancestors as they celebrate his rebirth: 'Avec eux, il pleura leur mort; mais aussi longuement, ils chantèrent sa naissance' (p.85).

By comparison, the passage in *La Maison au figuier* devoted to the *nuit du Coran* is a village festival, a collective celebration of the achievement of one individual in respect of a stage in Islamic education, a recognition of a change of status of that individual vis-à-vis the collectivity. Fadel Kane, in his analysis of the two passages, makes the contrast neatly: having referred, in the case of *L'Aventure ambiguë*, to 'un tableau chargé d'ombres, plein de solennité et dépouillé de tout ornement criard', he continues:

> Ici [dans *La Maison au figuier*], chants religieux, discours solennels, cadeaux somptueux, repas plantureux ont accompagné la récitation proprement dite du Coran par les trente récipiendiaires; là, le chevalier à la dalmatique et la mère de Samba Diallo étaient les seuls témoins de l'hommage que le fils a voulu rendre à ses parents et à la Parole de Dieu. (*32*, p.19)

In *la nuit du Coran*, the cold yet soft light of the stars is real, a feature of the real night sky, and yet it takes on a symbolic, almost metaphorical significance. Light and fire are constants in Kane's novel, bearing a multiplicity of meanings according to context, sometimes fully metaphoric, sometimes, as here, the symbolic use of natural phenomena (see *23* for a Bachelardian approach). It is surely significant that the majority of images, or instances of the symbolic use of language, occur either in passages referring to the *pays des Diallobé*, or at moments when a character, imbued with the spirit of the Diallobé, is reflecting on Western civilisation in negative fashion. The scenes in Paris, for instance, which have a much higher proportion of philosophical discourse, contain relatively few images. It would seem useful at this point to examine some of the images concerned, beginning with a further development of the phenomenon of light.

Radiant light has a positive significance, often indicating the presence of a spiritual force. Thus Samba Diallo, observing his father, notes his 'regard lumineux et calme' (p.106). This in a context where *le Chevalier* has just closed his Koran, and is clearly meditating on the Word. His son observes that 'Dieu lui est présence constante', resulting in a being who is removed from all extreme of passion, so much so that Samba draws the conclusion that surprises even him: 'Mon père ne vit pas, il prie...' The calm luminosity of his expression has been won only at the expense of purification by the element of fire: as his son reflects, 'Les prières profondes doivent incinérer dans l'homme toute exubérance profane de vie'. We shall return to this other, very important manifestation of light.

Another character whose expression is described as 'lumineux' is *la Grande Royale*, on her first appearance in the story, but to slightly different effect. The narrator tells us that 'un regard extraordinairement lumineux répandait sur cette figure un éclat impérieux' (p.31). The luminosity of her expression (denoting spirituality) is here extended into an 'éclat impérieux', denoting the immense authority of the woman – an authority apparently conquered through disciplined control of what might be interpreted as turbulent tendencies, and here conveyed again by the metaphor of fire, since towards the end of the same paragraph we read: 'Autour des yeux et sur les pommettes, sur tout le visage, il y avait comme le souvenir d'une jeunesse et d'une force sur lesquelles se serait apposé brutalement le rigide *éclat* d'un *souffle ardent*' (p.31; my emphasis).

When the term 'rayonnement' is used of Samba Diallo, the image is less complex, but the perception remains mysterious for the perceiver, Samba's new friend Jean Lacroix. In Monsieur N'Diaye's class, Jean is only dimly aware of Samba at first, conscious mainly of a 'trou de silence' in the classroom which he is suddenly able to attribute to Samba Diallo through 'une espèce de rayonnement contenu' (p.64). A little later we learn again that 'son visage rayonnait', and that Jean is convinced that if he looked at Samba Diallo he would perceive the answer to the teacher's question, 'tant son rayonnement était vif. [...] Mais lui, à part cette tension et ce rayonnement, ne bougeait pas'. Such repetition underlines the importance of this feature of Samba Diallo for the narrator, confirming firstly his otherness and secondly his intellectual, spiritual and social superiority, in spite of his youth.

Fire, that archetypal element, is used throughout the novel as a metaphor for purification, and as such is associated with the pain which necessarily has to be undergone on the road to salvation. The very name for the Koranic school, *le foyer ardent*, is an indication of this; as *la Grande Royale* says, 'sans la lumière des foyers nul ne peut rien pour le bien des Diallobé' (p.46), meaning that the spiritual element in the Diallobé culture must be guarded. It is the *maître* himself '[qui] a le feu qui embrase les disciples et éclaire le foyer' (p.75), providing therefore both purification and spiritual illumination. But it is also the *maître* who takes very literally his task of purifying his disciples through fire, when he attacks defaulters with burning fire-brands, as he does Samba Diallo in the opening scene of the novel (pp.15-16). The scene is set in the first lines, when the *maître* leaps as if he had walked on 'une des dalles incandescentes de la géhenne' as Samba Diallo makes a mistake in his recitation. The 'bûche ardente' used as the weapon of correction finds an echo in the 'lèvres ardentes' of Samba Diallo (p.15), and in the 'verset incandescent' (p.16) and the 'phrase étincelante' (p.14) which the child is finally able to recite with such passion.

Samba Diallo's vocation at this stage is initiation into the mysteries of the Muslim faith, and he knows that such initiation requires suffering. In addition, the boy, completely docile in the hands of his master, loves the Word of God for its mysterious beauty. 'Cette parole n'était pas comme les autres. C'était une parole que jalonnait la souffrance, c'était une parole venue de Dieu, elle était un miracle, elle était telle que Dieu lui-même l'avait prononcée' (p.14). We are invited therefore to interpret the symbolism of fire in this passage in a positive way. There are passages, however, where images of fire and light are used in a negative sense, to indicate an imitation, a glittering ersatz which lures the weak-minded soul away from its true destiny, this ersatz usually associated by the narrator with Western civilisation. The phenomenon is present from the very first contact with the West: the arrival of the coloniser is described in terms of an ambiguous dawn: 'Etrange aube! Le matin de l'Occident en Afrique noire fut constellé de sourires, de coups de canon et de verroteries brillantes' (p.59). The word 'constellé' announces the star-theme which, as we have seen, will be used to convey the sense of the spiritual, and of eternity. The newcomers announce themselves with both smiles and cannon-fire – both, however, having the same result, the subjection of the native population to the conqueror – but bear also 'verroteries brillantes', a term covering in literal terms all the bright trinkets used to 'buy' the Africans, but also, more generally, the gleaming but insubstantial ideas and artefacts of Western civilisation which will over the generations corrupt the values of African society.

A similar type of imagery is taken up by the *Chevalier*, on hearing that the Diallobé have decided that his son should go to the *école étrangère*. He is bitterly disappointed to think of his family '[qui] s'agenouillait devant l'éclat d'un feu d'artifice. Eclat solaire, il est vrai, éclat méridien d'une civilisation exaspérée', a sun which is in any case 'un mirage' (p.80). The Diallobé do not seem to realise that it is a 'course aveugle' in which they are engaging. The idea of the sun which blinds through its intensity is taken up again in the epilogue, when the Voice which greets Samba Diallo in the afterlife claims: 'soleils aveuglants de l'exil, vous êtes rêves oubliés' (p.189). To the burning sun of midday is preferred the sky at sunset, 'où de longues barres de rayons rouges joignaient le soleil agonisant à un zénith qu'envahissait une ombre insidieuse' (p.86) with all the metaphysical overtones of death and spiritual fulfilment we have already noted. The brilliant gleam of the ersatz is also evoked in this final chapter, when the Voice says to Samba Diallo: 'L'apparence et ses reflets brillent et pétillent', and asks him, 'Ne regretteras-tu pas l'apparence et ses reflets?' (p.188).

These 'reflets' are of the same nature as those which numbed the consciousness of *le fou*, and finally deranged him. In his account of his first experience in Europe, he refers to 'le carrelage [qui] étendait son miroir brillant où résonnait le claquement des souliers' (p.101), and later to 'le froid miroir glauque et brillant'. There is a strong echo here, of course, of the classic distinction made by the poets of *négritude*, whereby Europe is characterised by the hard, the brilliant, the metallic, the non-organic, whereas Africa is character-ised by the vegetal, the organic, the soil, things that are soft and pliant, things that grow.

The most nightmarish instance of the false brilliance of the imitation comes at the end of the *Chevalier*'s reflections already referred to above. Bitter at the Diallobé's submission to 'ce nouveau mal des ardents que l'Occident répand' (p.82), he has a sudden hallucination: 'Un point de notre globe brillait d'un éclat aveuglant, comme si un foyer immense y eût été allumé. Au cœur de ce brasier, un grouillement d'humains semblait se livrer à une incompréhensible et fantastique mimique d'adoration'. The light here is both strong and unhealthy: as the humans approach the fire's rays, they lose their original colour 'pour la blafarde teinte qui recouvrait tout alentour', the 'faux foyer', unlike the 'foyer ardent', having reduced all humankind to a single, undifferentiated mass.

Two final illustrations of the use of fire-imagery, where it is the danger of fire which is evoked, should be recalled here. Firstly, the striking image of the 'pays Diallobé [*sic*], désemparé, [qui] tournait sur lui-même comme un pur-sang pris dans un incendie' (p.22). Here, the Diallobé, caught in two minds as to the attitude to adopt to the *école étrangère*, are rendered panic-stricken and helpless, unable to make a move in any forwards direction. The other instance concerns Samba Diallo's fight with Demba, where the former strives to control his mounting anger: '[il] se surveillait, attentif à maîtriser cette vibration qui lui parcourait le corps, à dissiper cette odeur de feu de brousse qui lui chatouillait les narines' (p.29). It is the danger of the bush fire which is underlined here, the sense of impending catastrophe if the fire of his anger gets out of control. In neither case does fire represent a purifying element.

Another archetypal image, sometimes indeed found intermingling with that of fire, is the image of water. The importance of this element for the Tokolor, and its significance for their sense of the sacred, is stressed by Mamadou Wane, when he writes: 'Ces trois éléments du cosmos: terre, ciel et eau encadrant la structure sociétale en en déterminant les limites et la profondeur, conditionnent en dernière "instance" le sens de son historicité et la façon dont le sacré est à la fois pensé et vécu' (*73*, p.387). An association of water and fire can be found in the very first scene, which we have already considered in terms of fire-imagery when, having made up for his *lapsus*, Samba Diallo goes on to recite correctly the verse he had mispronounced: then, 'la Parole de Dieu coulait, pure et limpide, de ses lèvres ardentes' (p.15). Purification by fire allows passage for the liquid purity of the Word of God. The *maître*, holding the fire-brand and ready to strike again if necessary, listens to the child. 'Mais pendant que sa main menaçait, son regard avide admirait et son attention buvait la parole du garçonnet'.

The word of God, standing for all that is most precious in the Diallobé culture, is identified with fluidity elsewhere in the text. For example, the *maître*, meditating on the past and its incompatibility with the world with which he is now confronted, is 'réveillé au souvenir des temps évanouis où le pays vivait de Dieu et de la forte liqueur de ses traditions' (p.34). And in the same spirit, Samba Diallo, in Paris and far from his native land, reflects on the time when 'le savoir et la foi coulaient de source commune et grossissaient la même mer' (p.135), the sea standing here for universal wisdom, within Islam there being no distinction, no contradiction between science (in the West usually looked on as profane) and faith. A similar instance of an all-encompassing spiritual element in which Samba Diallo, as a disciple at the *foyer ardent*, was bathed, is illustrated again by him, and again from his Paris exile: beset by doubt, he addresses himself to God, recalling 'comme tu nourrissais mon existence de la tienne. [...] Je te sentais la mer profonde d'où s'épandait ma pensée et en même temps qu'elle, tout. Par toi, j'étais le même flot que tout' (p.139).

As we noted in respect of fire, the water element is not always totally metaphorical, and this is particularly true with regard to *le fleuve*, a very important physical reality in the *pays des Diallobé*, on which the life of the community depended in a very material sense. The Senegal River is impressive at any stage of the year: during the *hivernage* (the rainy season) it must have struck awe in the heart of Samba Diallo's creator. When the boy goes to the *école étrangère*, asked by Jean Lacroix about his origins, he replies immediately: 'Nous venons des bords d'un grand fleuve' (p.70) – proof if any were needed that language does not need to use imagery in order to be impressive. Thus Samba Diallo, returning home from Paris, is transfixed by the sound of the river, to which his perceptions give an almost mythological status:

> On n'entendait que la grande voix du fleuve, répercutée
> par ses berges vertigineuses. Samba Diallo tourna son
> regard vers cette voix et vit, au loin, la falaise d'argile. Il
> se souvint qu'en son enfance, il avait longtemps cru que

cette immense crevasse partageait l'univers en deux
parties que soudait le fleuve. (p.184)

In this way, when the voice of the river is used as an image, it is
immeasurably more effective for being rooted in reality. For example,
the fusion of Samba Diallo's voice with that of the river during the
nuit du Coran gains in heightened emotional charge and pathos as a
result of this association:

Il lui sembla que sa voix était devenue innombrable et
sourde comme celle du fleuve certains soirs.
   Mais la voix du fleuve était moins véhémente et aussi
moins près des larmes. La voix du fleuve ne charriait pas
ce refus dramatique que maintenant il criait. Elle n'avait
pas non plus l'accompagnement de fond de cette mélopée
nostalgique. (p.85)

The river is equally present in the epilogue which, this time, is
not just the end of an era as in the passage just quoted, but an
extremely complex representation of the after-life into which Samba
Diallo enters when killed by the insane gesture of *le fou*. The dead
soul and *la voix* which greets him are firstly presented as valley and
river, at the beginning of the *hivernage*: 'Délicieux accueil que fait la
vallée desséchée au flot revenu, tu réjouis le flot' (p.188). And again,
'Où es-tu? Je ne te vois plus. Il n'y a que cette turgescence qui sourd
en moi, comme fait l'eau nouvelle dans le fleuve en crue' (p.189), the
new waters underlining the fact of the soul's rebirth into a different
and superior condition. 'Le fleuve monte! Je déborde...' (p.190), and
Samba Diallo experiences again the sense, present in the *pays des
Diallobé*, but lost during his Western exile, of being entirely suffused
by the divine element (see p.139). The realm where he finds himself
is beyond opposition, beyond ambiguity; time is reduced to an
instant, but '[un] instant qui dure. [...] Au cœur de l'instant, voici que
l'homme est immortel, car l'instant est infini.' Thus the instant and
the flow of thought are identified: 'L'instant est le lit du fleuve de ma
pensée.' From river, the flow becomes the sea: 'Dans la mer du
temps, l'instant porte l'image du profil de l'homme' (*ibid.*). The soul,

at last 'in its element', greets the sea joyfully: 'La mer! Voici la mer!
Salut à toi, sagesse retrouvée, ma victoire! La limpidité de ton flot est
attente de mon regard' (p.191). Water and luminosity come together
in this final passage, as the soul, taking in the eternal element that the
sea represents, affirms: 'Je te regarde, et tu reluis, sans limites'. The
Sufi context of these images is made explicit by Lings, when he
writes:

> From time to time a Revelation 'flows' like a great tidal
> wave from the Ocean of Infinitude to the shores of our
> finite world; and Sufism is the vocation and the discipline
> and the science of plunging into the ebb of one of these
> waves and being drawn back with it to its Eternal and
> Infinite Source. (*59*, p.11)

After these considerations on the status and use of language in
L'Aventure ambiguë, can one make any firm statement regarding the
enterprise of conveying through one language the culture of another?
Is it possible 'd'apprivoiser avec des mots de France, / Ce cœur qui
m'est venu du Sénégal', as Léon Laleau so memorably put it? The
writer and critic Léon Nadjo belives that it is, on two conditions:

> l'écrivain doit être imprégné de son identité culturelle et
> aussi avoir pris conscience de son mode d'expression le
> plus naturel, c'est-à-dire des tendances linguistiques et
> stylistiques de la communauté culturelle dont il fait
> partie. Il lui faut ensuite privilégier ces tendances dans
> toute autre langue où il voudrait exprimer son âme, ce qui
> suppose, de sa part, la connaissance parfaite – c'est la
> seconde condition – de cette langue. (*66*, p.103)

'To be an artist is to fail', as Beckett wrote. But insofar as
success is possible, it would seem that Cheikh Hamidou Kane, by
fulfilling admirably Nadjo's two conditions of acute consciousness of
cultural identity and perfect mastery of the French language, has
succeeded.

4. The Conflict of Cultures

The cultural debate is at the heart of *L'Aventure ambiguë*. The crisis provoked by the presence of an alien occupant, here concretised in the dilemma concerning the *école nouvelle*, is admirably expressed by *le Chef*, when he asks: 'peut-on apprendre ceci sans oublier cela, et ce qu'on apprend vaut-il ce qu'on oublie?' (p.44). Against critics who felt that the fight against colonialist oppression was underplayed in *L'Aventure ambiguë*, Cheikh Hamidou Kane affirms that:

> le problème le plus important qu'il fallait élucider pour moi lorsque j'écrivais ce livre [...] était le problème des conflits de cultures: d'une culture traditionnelle, en l'occurence [*sic*] d'une culture africaine, noire et musulmane, avec la culture, disons, du colonisateur. Donc l'aspect politique n'est pas absent de *L'Aventure ambiguë*, mais l'aspect culturel m'a paru plus essentiel, et plus déterminant. (*10*)

This is of course why, in addition, there is no mention of the Second World War in the text, why the debate surrounding the development of Islam, contemporary to the events of the novel nevertheless, figures nowhere.

In the literary fiction which Kane has created, the issue of cultural confrontation acquires at times tragic proportions: regarding his own situation, the writer admits to it being a question of existential significance, in that he experiences his position between two worlds as 'très douloureuse' (*12*). On the other hand, he remains forward-looking and realistic: the question is, what action is possible, given the situation we find ourselves in? The presence, the all-pervasive influence of the Other, is inescapable: globalisation in all its guises is a necessary part of the future, and it is a matter of accommodating *ce monde nouveau* without losing one's essential identity (*ibid.*). Interestingly, Kane cites the West as an example of what is at stake: in the lecture published in *Esprit*, he wonders whether the current problems of the West do not spring from a crisis of identity: 'l'Occident est pris d'inquiétude: et s'il avait été dupe? et si, acquérant ceci, il avait du même mouvement perdu autre chose, d'aussi essentiel à sa vie?' (*3*, p.397).

The question formula of the above is typical. The debate continues. And debate implies dialogue. Hence the form of a substantial part of *L'Aventure ambiguë*, which is unusual for the African novel in its relative lack of description and its emphasis on dialogue: the epilogue in fact becomes exclusively dialogue between the dead soul and the welcoming Voice. It is possible to see further influence of the oral tradition at work here: as we saw in the previous chapter, in a traditional society, all problems are evoked via the word, all matters are resolved through the word. Debate is the essential means of moving society forward. In a speech given when Minister for Development, Kane picks up the Dogon myth identifying the word with weaving: dialogue, he says, does not proceed 'fil à fil', but is a question of warp and weft, 'où chacun a part au dialogue de tous' (*4*), and the same image is evoked in *L'Aventure ambiguë* by *le maître*, when he says: 'La Parole tisse ce qui est, plus intimement que la lumière ne tisse le jour' (p.131). The preponderance of dialogue is also a function of the dramatisation of the material: far from being abstract discussions between disembodied characters, the scenes of philosophical debate are *mises en scène* as in the oral tradition, where description is unnecessary because members of the 'audience', that is the community itself, have the characters, and the setting, in front of them. It should be noted also that this method of writing conforms to the genre of the *récit*, in which narrative presence is at a minimum: characters present themselves from the inside, and the narration remains discreet and unobtrusive.

Because of the importance of dialogue, the characters are made to bear a large part of the weight of the significance of the novel. They do this, however, more as representative of points of view, than as individuals. But inasmuch as the author is committed to the ambiguity of his theme, and convinced that there are no solutions to the dilemma in this life, he is in a certain sense in all his characters. (Goré characterises the writing as 'un dialogue intime d'une conscience avec elle-même', *28*, p.73.) Hence perhaps the great evenness of presentation: there is no distinction between 'good' and 'bad' characters. Even when a character is putting forward a point of view which is antipathetic to the narrator, that character is presented sympathetically. Characters are exemplary, as in a medieval allegory: they have a hieratic quality, and are subject to great physical and moral stylisation (*25*, p.478). Other critics have noted the symbolic, emblematic nature of many of the names: *le Chevalier*, *le Maître*, *le Chef*, *le Fou*, *la Grande Royale* are names which characterise rather than individualise (*22*, p.189). Among critics, Vincent Monteil was the first to suggest a comparison with the game of chess (*1*, p.9) and certainly opposition of characters bearing symbolic weight plays a role here. The idea of chess-pieces could also prove fertile in the sense that the characters are moved from the outside, as it were by the hand of God. What is certain is that stylisation of character contributes greatly to the tragic universalism with which Kane wished to imbue his novel.

In order to elucidate the debate, then, let us look in closer detail at the presentation of character, beginning with the young hero himself, Samba Diallo. He represents firstly the Diallobé aristocracy, the *toorodbe* leaders of Tokolor society, and his fundamental nature is defined by his place in the hierarchy. Social status is conferred by birth, and in a world that recalls at times that of Corneille, to be 'well born' implies at the same time a certain moral perfection. The situation is well expressed by Boubacar Ly, when he writes: 'Chacun [...] dans ces sociétés a conscience de la place qu'il occupe dans la hiérarchie sociale et de prestige (son rang social) et cherche à réaliser le "fonds moral" de ce rang' (*60*, p.44). All his life, therefore, Samba Diallo will be concerned with *becoming* what he *is*. Within the hierarchical society into which he is born, the situation is entirely static: the only movement is in the adjustment to the behaviour expected of the individual, according to his rank. Hence a certain passivity detectable in Samba Diallo: he expects no say in his destiny, and accepts unquestioningly the fate decided for him by the community. As a young boy he feels the burden of his noble origins (pp.26-27), but not in any sense that he feels inclined or free to shed them. As in allegory or folk-tale, his physical portrait corresponds to what he is: at the *foyer ardent*, the rags he wears as a *talibé* are unable to disguise his birth: 'Il ne se passait pas de jour que quelqu'un ne fît de remarque sur la noblesse de son port ou sur l'élégance racée de son maintien, en dépit des haillons sordides dont il se couvrait' (p.27). The narrator speaks of 'le fin visage de l'enfant' (p.15), and describes him as 'tout en lignes longues et nerveuses' (p.28). By contrast, the peasant Demba, again faithful to his origins, 'était plutôt rondelet, paisible et immobile'.

If Samba Diallo represents traditional Tokolor society, he also represents the influence of Islam on that society. For Cheikh Hamidou Kane, the two are indissociable, and he takes the Islamic Futa as paradigmatic for the whole of sub-Saharan Africa. But in practice, the balance between the Tokolor rulers and the Sufi *marabouts* has been a delicate one. Islam was used by the *toorodbe* to justify their position, but traditional Sufi suspicion of temporal power meant that their support could never be taken for granted (*30*, p.289). In *L'Aventure ambiguë*, this is expressed in Thierno's attempt to kill in Samba Diallo 'la morgue des Diallobé' (p.32). Thierno is conscious that 'au fond de toute noblesse, il est un fond de paganisme. La noblesse est l'exaltation de l'homme, la foi est avant tout humilité, sinon humiliation' (p.33). Samba Diallo himself bows willingly to this discipline: he accepts the nobility of his birth, but would prefer 'une noblesse plus discrète, plus authentique, non point acquise mais conquise durement et qui fût plus spirituelle que temporelle' (p.27). When *la Grande Royale* intervenes against Thierno's harsh treatment of the boy, she is thus trying to protect him from himself as much as from Thierno; but she is also exemplifying an age-old conflict between the secular and the religious power in the Futa (*27*, pp.33-34).

Samba Diallo is at the centre of this conflict; but he is also the Diallobé's chosen representative in the conflict with the coloniser (see *30*), in that it is he who is chosen to attend the *école nouvelle*, an experience which initially delights him through its immediate appeal to his understanding, before ultimately breaking him (for further detail, see *33*). The conflict is shown in two stages: firstly the debate, centred on the school, which is in reality a debate about how to come to terms, in as beneficial a way as possible, with the new world that has been opened up to Diallobé society; secondly, the effect of Western schooling on Samba Diallo, and his progressive alienation. The attractions of the school are made clear: it is the 'aimant' which comes after the initial 'canons': 'Le canon contraint les corps, l'école fascine les âmes' (p.60). In the words which Vercors gives to his German officer in *Le Silence de la mer*: 'Pour conquérir suffit la force: pas pour dominer. Nous savons très bien qu'une armée n'est rien pour dominer.' Georges Hardy, the noted Directeur de l'Enseignement en A.O.F., made the same distinction when he indicated that the initial military conquest of Africa '[doit] se doubler d'une nouvelle conquête du pays et des habitants'. The coloniser wanted to 'posséder jusqu'au cœur de nos sujets', with the ultimate object of the 'nouvelle conquête' being: 'Mise en valeur du pays, attachement raisonné de l'indigène à notre œuvre [...]. Conquête moins rapide et brillante que la première, mais aussi féconde et méritoire, et dont l'instrument ne peut être que l'école' (*53*, pp.2-3). The image of the magnet used by the narrator has to take into account also, however, the fact that neither the coloniser nor the colonised initially wanted the other. The school is a 'necessary means' for both:

> L'homme ne veut pas de l'école parce qu'elle lui impose,
> pour vivre – c'est-à-dire pour être libre, pour se nourrir,
> pour s'habiller – de passer désormais par ses bancs;
> l'école ne veut pas davantage de l'homme parce qu'il lui
> impose pour survivre – c'est-à-dire pour s'étendre et
> prendre racine où sa nécessité l'a débarquée – de compter
> avec lui. (p.61)

The coloniser has a need of people with sufficient instruction to act as intermediaries between the imposed system and the native population: the motivation of the coloniser is above all practical. In order to accomplish this, instruction in the French language is crucial; and here, the ideological joins the pragmatic: with the French language, 'c'est la civilisation qui arrive et qui transforme la barbarie' (Victor Duruy, quoted *65*, p.91). Throughout the literature relating to the imposition of French schooling on Africa, whether 'assimilationniste' or 'associationniste', benignly paternalistic or arrogantly authoritarian, there is the same refrain: Africa is the 'Dark Continent', peopled with savages who have no history and no civilisation. In the case of some of the peoples of Africa, these bullying tactics created a crisis of confidence from which they are still trying to recover. In the case of the Tokolor, the coloniser reckoned without the strong sense of identity possessed by this people, and also, most particularly, without the overwhelming influence of Islamic culture. As David Robinson says, 'Islam provided a kind of cultural identity for West Africans that balanced the strong ethnocentric superiority of the French' (*67*, pp.122-23).

In the case of Samba Diallo, however, the strong Islamic culture he had received from his earliest days is a major element in his disorientation. He proves 'inassimilable', he becomes a hybrid being who, because his native Islamic culture is at odds with the Western civilisation towards which in certain respects he feels a strong attraction, no longer belongs to one or to the other. From an exclusively collective environment, where society defines what the individual is and therefore what he can do, Samba Diallo confronts the world of the individual, where, turned loose on a sea of conflicting possibilities, he is expected to make personal decisions which refer to no fixed value system. As Victor Bol puts it: 'Le vrai drame, bien plus que dans la contingence des événements, c'est là qu'il se passe; dans le passage brusque du monde du sacré à celui de l'individu qu'est l'Occident' (*44*, p.134). The moment in Paris, when he receives the letter from the *chef des Diallobé*, which is a sort of philosophical meditation on the problems confronting the Diallobé, is deeply significant: he is sufficiently alienated, 'Westernised' by this time, to react negatively: 'Que me font leurs problèmes? J'ai le droit de faire comme ce vieil homme [*maître Thierno*], de me retirer de l'arène où s'enchevêtrent leurs désirs, leurs infirmités, leur chair, de me retirer au-dedans de moi-même' (p.138). Such a reaction would have been unthinkable to a Diallobé who had not been through the *école étrangère*: 'Croire ce que ne croit pas son père, c'est déroger de la règle de conduite, de bon sens, c'est errer dans la nuit athée des Blancs' (*56*, p.97). But what seems like an acknowledgement of individual responsibility is in fact, in this case, a recognition of impotence.

Samba Diallo is a highly complex, tragic character, therefore, representative of a double heritage, pulled both between the two strands of that heritage, and between those and a third element represented by the coloniser.

Thierno, *le maître des Diallobé*, has no such complexity. He represents orthodox Muslim and Sufi values, which have no answer other than retrenchment to the challenge issued by the West. The latest in a long line of '[*maîtres des Diallobé* qui] étaient aussi les maîtres que le tiers du continent se choisissait pour guides sur la voie de Dieu en même temps que dans les affaires humaines' (p.22), his capacity to legislate for 'les affaires humaines' seems impotent at this juncture, when the order of society had to take into account an alien conqueror. At the beginning of the novel, we see him in a commanding spiritual position, exacting total fidelity to the Word of God from his disciples. But he admits to the deputation come to seek guidance relating to the *école nouvelle* that he is the guide only for their children, and not for society as a whole (p.95). To their pleas for a clear answer, he replies: 'Vous attendez que ce que je vous dirai indique ce que vous ferez, comme dix indique onze à celui qui compte bien, n'est-ce pas? [...] je vous jure que je ne sais rien de semblable. Autant que vous, je voudrais savoir' (p.97).

Le maître represents death in two different yet interrelated ways. Firstly, he is committed to the mortification of the flesh, his own and that of his disciples, in the higher interests of the spirit. Secondly, he represents a dying world: if the Diallobé do not find a way of exploiting the technical secrets of the West, by compromising with the coloniser through the new school, the *foyer ardent* will be extinguished, and there will be no more pupils. In addition, everything for which he has lived will be destroyed, since 'la misère est ennemi de Dieu', and people in their destitution will turn from God. Accordingly, everything about his physical appearance speaks of death. He is described as 'vieux, maigre et émacié, tout desséché par ses macérations' (p.17). 'Ses jarrets étaient devenus secs et rigides comme le bois mort que brûlaient les disciples' (p.39), and when he tries to kneel down, 'le grand âge et les rhumatismes avaient fait de ce geste [...] cette gymnastique grotesque et pénible que l'assistance émue suivait en haletant' (p.130). He dies before the end of the novel, and to mark the significance of the end of an era, he chooses Demba, the canny, pragmatic peasant, to take on the turban of *le maître*.

Le Chef represents to a large extent the same values. The narrator tells us that he and *le maître* resemble each other in nature, and have a natural affinity (p.42). No more than *le maître*, does *le Chef* know how to guide his people out of their dilemma. 'Je suis une pauvre chose qui tremble et qui ne sait pas.' The dialogue between the two men understandably does not get very far towards a solution, although *le Chef* in particular understands only too well the problem. 'Les Diallobé voulaient plus de poids' (p.43), 'le poids' representing materiality and physical well-being, as against the spiritual, ascetic values of *le maître*. The dilemma, as expressed by *le Chef* is therefore: 'Comment donner aux Diallobé la connaissance des arts et l'usage des armes, la possession de la richesse et la santé du corps sans les alourdir en même temps?' (pp.44-45). But he is better at expressing the dilemma than at resolving it: as *la Grande Royale* puts it, 'Mon frère n'est pas un prince. [...] C'est un sage' (p.31), a thinker and contemplative rather than a man of political action and decisiveness. He is nevertheless a sympathetic character, humble and compassionate. In the words of Moriceau and Rouch, 'Si le chef n'est pas la figure primordiale de *L'Aventure ambiguë*, il en est peut-être, avec le chevalier, la plus humaine' (*20*, p.23).

It is *la Grande Royale* who intervenes in the debate between the two men and injects an element of realism. We have already had occasion to evoke the remarkable portrait of this woman, real and yet emblematic, drawn by the narrator. Her physical appearance bears witness to her social and moral status. We see her for the first time when she breaks up the fight between Samba Diallo and Demba (p.30): she is impressively tall, young-looking for her age (she needs the weight of years to give her moral stature, but she needs to wear them lightly), clad in a long blue gown and white veil which reveals only her face, 'qui était comme une page vivante de l'histoire du pays des Diallobé. Tout ce que le pays compte de tradition épique s'y lisait' (p.31). She is immediately pronounced therefore as standing for Diallobé society as a whole, rather than simply an individual. She is represented also as symbolising the ideal submission of aristocratic pride to Islam when the narrator comments: 'L'Islam refrénait la redoutable turbulence de [ses] traits, de la même façon que la voilette les enserrait'.

She represents power, nonetheless, but also the lucidity and intelligence necessary to retain it. As Cheikh Hamidou Kane himself expresses it, speaking of his aunt:

> Elle n'en revenait pas de la défaite des Diallobé, et donc de la défaite des Peuls, et de tous les Hal-pulaar [...] devant les armes des Blancs et en l'occurrence du colonisateur français, parce qu'elle avait l'impression que sa culture et sa civilisation étaient d'une qualité telle qu'elle ne pourrait pas comprendre qu'on l'ait défaite. Mais, assez rapidement, comme c'était une personne intelligente, elle a compris qu'on ne pouvait vivre isolé, qu'il fallait composer avec le monde qui venait à nous. (*12*)

In a word, the Diallobé had to go to the enemy camp, 'apprendre chez eux l'art de vaincre sans avoir raison' (p.47). (Interestingly, Malraux puts an almost identical argument into the mouth of one of the characters in *La Condition humaine*, Tiémoko, when he says: 'Il ne s'agit pas d'avoir raison, mais de vaincre.') This attitude is not mere cynicism, however, as Kane explains:

> La fameuse exhortation de la Grande Royale a un contenu à la fois moral et politique. Elle considérait [...] et avec elle notre société toute [*sic*] entière, que ce que fait l'homme doit être orienté par la volonté de faire le bien, par exemple, celle d'édifier une société, de l'instruire, de la soigner, de lui donner un confort; mais en même temps, il doit le faire dans une perspective de vérité et de justice. (*9*, p.83)

In her notable address to the Diallobé people, she calls for sacrifice on the part of the adults, so that Diallobé society may live on in their children: using images taken from the natural cycle of foodplants, seed-time and harvest, she represents life and vigour against the inevitable death of the world of *le maître* (p.57). She is the Jungian archetypal Mother, whose concern is for the future of the tribe (*25*, p.480).

Le Fou is, in respect of the Diallobé, the exact opposite of *la Grande Royale*, insofar as his reaction to the alien culture with which he has come into contact has been total rejection. He is representative of traditional Islam, finding only in *le maître* the solace of someone to understand him. Kane himself goes one step further in his current explanation of the character, seeing in him the dangers of intransigence and Islamic fundamentalism. Samba Diallo finds himself confronted with

> quelqu'un qui avait suivi ou même subi le même parcours que lui, mais sans avoir disposé des mêmes atouts, du même temps pour juger [...] quelqu'un qui a été un soldat, [...] qui avait été recruté dans l'armée des tirailleurs sénégalais, qui donc n'avait pas été à l'école, mais on l'avait pris tel qu'il était, on l'a extrait de son village, et après une formation assez brève, on l'avait envoyé en Europe dans un des conflits européens auxquels les tirailleurs sénégalais ont participé, [...] lorsque cet homme-là a subi cette expérience traumatisante, il en est revenu en se disant que si c'est cela l'Occident il valait mieux ne pas aller en direction de cette société occidentale. (*16*)

Kane speaks of his 'réflexe de crispation identitaire' which turns him in on himself, affecting his sense of Muslim identity so that in the end 'il était pour une pratique extrêmement fanatique et intransigeante, intégriste, finalement, fermée de l'Islam' (*ibid.*; see also *11*, p.134). This critical view of *le fou* is that presented in *Les Gardiens du temple*, where his death-sentence for the killing of Samba Diallo is evoked, a sentence subsequently commuted because of his mental instability (*2*, p.51). In the novel, he is a poignant but sympathetic figure, his loss of hold on reality symbolised by the double contradiction of his refusal to accept either the death of *le maître* or the fact that Samba Diallo is not his successor. As with other characters, his physical portrait is deeply telling, his inability to harmonise the traditional world of the Diallobé with the West as he discovered it symbolised by the military great-coat incongruously covering in part his African attire, 'laissant une impression hétéroclite' (p.98). Although Kane subsequently emphasises his war-experience, in the novel this experience is questioned by his fellow-Diallobé, and it is rather his initial contact with Western civilisation itself, in all its cold, mechanical brutality, that is highlighted, making his criticism of the inhumanity of that civilisation all the more universal and relevant (see pp.100-05).

Leaving on one side for a moment the central figure of *le Chevalier*, there are a number of more or less important minor characters, who represent various aspects of the fundamental dilemma, and who act as sounding-boards for the main characters, or play the role of confidant as in Classical tragedy (see *18*, p.35).

Outside the world of the Diallobé, the one character representing traditional, spiritual values, is *le pasteur*, M. Martial. Physically, his bearing indicates rectitude, strength, a life devoted to essentials and to the truth. Strangely, his 'front large' recalls for Samba Diallo that of *le maître des Diallobé*, 'à la peau raccornie par les longues prosternations' (p.122). His identity as a European indicates Kane's refusal to see the cultural divide as simply a black-white issue, although his conflict with his superiors would indicate that he held minority views regarding missionary activity. His project, which was refused, was to go out to Africa bearing only the Word of God (it is significant that he is a Protestant, Protestantism being the religion of the Book), unsupported by the material assets of medicine or technology. As he explains, 'notre tâche étant d'évangéliser, j'eusse évité d'emporter jusqu'au médicament le moins encombrant et le plus utile' (p.127). In the scene between him, his daughter Lucienne and Samba Diallo, it is clear that he and the young African understand one another implicitly, the odd one out being Lucienne.

She makes a fairly brief appearance, but is an important figure, representing the views of Marxist materialism. The narrator gives us no detailed physical portrait of Samba Diallo's fellow-student, but various references present her as typically European: he mentions her 'regard bleu' (p.149), she is his 'blonde camarade' (p.152), and at the height of one of their debates we learn that: 'les grands yeux bleus de Lucienne fixaient Samba Diallo de toute leur immensité. Le visage n'était plus, autour des yeux, qu'une vague auréole blanche, rose, et blonde' (p.153). It is a purely intellectual relationship, but one in which, in spite of their differences, there is great mutual respect. But whereas Samba Diallo is deeply divided, indecisive, Lucienne's position seems clear: as Samba Diallo says to her, 'de ton propre aveu, lorsque tu auras libéré le dernier prolétaire de sa misère, que tu l'auras réinvesti de dignité, tu considéreras que ton œuvre est achevée' (pp.153-54). Samba Diallo's implied criticism of Lucienne's position is reflected in a comment of V.Y. Mudimbe: 'Une civilisation commence à déchoir à partir du moment où la vie devient son unique obsession' (*83*, p.99).

Another representative of Western materialism, and at the same time of colonialism, is Paul Lacroix, the colonial administrator. Notable for the impressive debate which he provokes with *le Chevalier* (pp.86-93), he represents the Western scientific approach, and is impatient and to a certain extent uncomprehending of the Sufi metaphysics of *le Chevalier*. But it is noteworthy that he is again treated sympathetically, that he treats his interlocutor with respect (not invariably the case among colonial administrators), and the reader is invited to take his intellectual position seriously.

A final cluster of minor characters revolves around the person of Pierre-Louis, the retired West Indian lawyer whom Samba Diallo meets in Paris. A powerful, sceptical figure, he reflects the viewpoint of *la Grande Royale* to the extent that his professional life has been dedicated to fighting the enemy with his own weapons. Through a thorough knowledge of French law, he has been able to defend numerous compatriots with a 'passion révolutionnaire' which recalls the 'souffle [de] Saint-Just' (p.146). His two sons, 'le capitaine Hubert' and Marc, an engineer, and his wife, 'la princesse baguée', are present to stimulate Samba Diallo's reflections rather than to represent a particular point of view, but Adèle, Hubert's daughter, plays a more important role. She is given a more detailed – and flattering – physical description than any other minor character (p.158), and is the only female character towards whom Samba Diallo feels any sentimental attraction, although this is quickly repressed (p.160). Her main function in the dialogue springs from her status as 'déracinée': born on the banks of the Seine, she has no *pays des Diallobé* to turn to in order to establish her roots. But she spontaneously understands Samba Diallo's feelings of exile in Paris, declaring: 'Ici, tout est tellement aride' (p.169). This in turn provokes the young African's inward reflection: 'Sentirait-elle vraiment "l'exil", cette fille née aux bords de la Seine? Cependant, elle n'a jamais connu qu'eux. Et son oncle Marc? A mes premiers mots, ils se sont reconnus des nôtres. Le soleil de leur savoir ne peut-il vraiment rien à l'ombre de notre peau?'

If, in our consideration of the various characters in the novel, we have left Samba Diallo's father, *le Chevalier*, to the end, it is partly because of his stature as a character, but partly also because he seems to have both a grasp of the dilemma, and some kind of vision of a solution. Kane's own father, whom the fictional character apparently closely resembles, was, it seems, a man of very broad culture and sympathies, whom Kane greatly admired. He sees him as having been 'more African' than himself and, with his more extensive knowledge of African languages, 'son africanité était plus profonde que la mienne':

> En outre, mon père [...] avait une culture religieuse musulmane beaucoup plus profonde que la mienne. Car il avait réussi à sauvegarder dans cette culture religieuse musulmane notre culture traditionnelle qui n'est pas incompatible avec le dogme islamique. [...] Enfin mon père [...] a su tirer de l'Occident l'essentiel de sa culture. [...] Il savait ce qu'il y avait d'essentiel et d'important là-dedans et il savait en même temps écarter ce qui était accessoire. (*11*, p.136).

In a word, it seems that he had succeeded in reconciling the three-cornered dilemma that Samba Diallo found himself at the heart of, that between traditional culture, Islam, and the West.

In the novel, the physical portrait of the fictionalised character is drawn by the young Jean Lacroix, when he sees him for the first time:

> L'homme était grand [...]. Les boubous qu'il portait étaient blancs et amples. On sentait sous ses vêtements une stature puissante mais sans empâtement. Les mains étaient grandes et fines tout à la fois. La tête, qu'on eût dit découpée dans du grès noir et brillant, achevait, par son port, de lui donner une posture hiératique. (p.66)

Looking at him, Jean cannot help thinking of 'certaine gravure de ses manuels d'histoire représentant un chevalier du Moyen Age revêtu de sa dalmatique'. The impression created is timeless, full of authority and gravitas. But his smile as he greets Jean overflows with warmth and charisma: 'son visage, son beau visage d'ombre serti de clarté, lui souriait.'

His position regarding the dilemma of the Diallobé is not straightforward, however, perhaps precisely because of his experience of both traditional and Western culture. Although he has necessarily been to the *école étrangère* (he works for the colonial administration), he is very reluctant to send his son there, and bows only to the superior collective authority of the community as a whole, led by *la Grande Royale*. It seems to be the indecent haste in the traditional world's embrace of the West, 'leur course aveugle' (p.80), '[le] délire d'occidentalisation' (pp.81-82) that distresses him. What the world needs is not 'un regain d'accélération' but 'un lit sur lequel, s'allongeant, son âme décidera une trêve' (p.80). 'L'équilibre' is the mark of civilisation: 'Est-il de civilisation hors l'équilibre de l'homme et sa disponibilité? L'homme civilisé, n'est-ce pas l'homme disponible? Disponible pour aimer son semblable, pour aimer Dieu surtout'. But he recognises at the same time the physical, material needs that are pressing ever more urgently upon his people: the conflicting voices of the Sufi mystic and the man with responsibilities for his people make themselves heard: 'La matière dont [l'homme] participe par son corps – que tu hais – le harcèle d'une cacophonie de demandes auxquelles il faut qu'il réponde'. 'La civilisation est une

architecture de réponses. Sa perfection, comme celle de toute
demeure, se mesure au confort que l'homme y éprouve, à l'appoint de
liberté qu'elle lui procure' (p.81). But, he admits, the Diallobé are not
free, and he desires their freedom. 'Mais l'esclavage de l'homme
parmi une forêt de solutions vaut-il mieux aussi?'

So much for the problem. In his dialogue with Paul Lacroix,
after the initial presentation of traditional Muslim teachings on the
purpose of life and its eschatology or final ends, he gives his views on
the point at which civilisation has arrived, and makes a projection
into a new world not yet born. In a sense, he says, the end of the
world has already arrived, since 'l'ère des destinées singulières est
révolue. [...] nul ne peut plus vivre de la seule préservation de soi'
(p.92). This 'end of the world' was made inevitable by the intrusion
of the coloniser, since when the process has been inexorable. But this
enforced 'globalisation' has given a role to the developing nations
('nous tous, dégingandés et lamentables, nous les sous-développés,
qui nous sentons gauches en un monde de parfait ajustement
mécanique', p.93). Le Chevalier accepts this vision of the future,
which his son will help to build, 'non plus en étranger venu des
lointains, mais en artisan responsable des destinées de la cité' (p.92).
Playing with the images of light and shade which have been a feature
of their dialogue, Lacroix says: 'Il nous enseignera les secrets de
l'ombre', to which le Chevalier replies: 'La cité future, grâce à mon
fils, ouvrira ses baies sur l'abîme, d'où viendront de grandes bouffées
d'ombre sur nos corps desséchés, sur nos fronts altérés.' The role of
traditional societies is thus to bring an element of spirituality, of
metaphysical Angst, to the global civilisation yet to be constructed, in
order to counter the certainties of the world 'de parfait ajustement
mécanique'.

We can now see the reason for le Chevalier's hesitancy at
sending his son to school. The Diallobé can fulfil the role traced for
them only if they remain authentic and faithful to themselves,
whereas le Chevalier knows only too well from his own experience
that Samba Diallo risks losing this cultural fidelity through l'école
étrangère.

It is important to note that, for Kane, the cultural divergence
discernible today between the developed and the developing world is

a fairly recent phenomenon. Samba Diallo opines that the history of the West 'avait subi un accident qui l'a gauchie et, finalement, sortie de son projet' (p.126). The 'projet', which in the West remained the same up until Pascal, 'c'est encore le projet de toute la pensée non occidentale'. With Descartes things altered: 'Non qu'ils se soient préoccupés de problèmes différents, mais qu'ils s'en soient occupés différemment. [...] Descartes est plus parcimonieux dans sa quête; si, grâce à cette modestie et aussi à sa méthode, il obtient plus de réponses, ce qu'il apporte nous concerne moins aussi, et nous est de peu de secours.' In the lecture published in *Esprit*, Kane speaks of 'la profonde fraternité d'origine et de destin' linking the West with the developing world (*3*, p.376), suggesting that it is an obsession with 'la raison discursive' that has provoked the 'aberration' (*3*, p.385). Because of this common ancestry, however, it would seem that Kane is hopeful of a reconciliation of cultures in the future.

To what extent is this vision of a 'civilisation de l'universel' a parallel with that of Senghor and the concept of *négritude*? There clearly are similarities: both Senghor and Kane are convinced of the importance of the contribution of developing nations to this civilisation not yet born. As Senghor puts it, 'La civilisation du XXIe siècle – que prépare celle d'aujourd'hui – [...] sera *humanisme* ou *barbarie* selon que les peuples du Tiers Monde, et parmi eux les peuples noirs, y auront apporté leurs contributions' (*70*, p.242). Both writers are equally convinced of the value of 'métissage'. Kane's particular vision of *négritude* 'accepte un dialogue nouveau et ne refuse pas l'ambiguïté des métissages, puisqu'elle se sent capable enfin de les assumer, donc de les dépasser. Elle ne rejettera donc pas la part de l'Occident en elle...' (*4*, p.30). Either facet of the 'métissage' is by itself sterile: as Pierre Fougeyrollas says:

> Entre le traditionalisme intégral dont l'impuissance est claire pour beaucoup d'entre eux, et le consentement total à l'occidentalisation qui en tente un certain nombre sans les satisfaire suffisamment, il y a la recherche, difficile mais exaltante, d'un devenir socio-culturel originel et inventif, capable d'emprunter à la traditionalité et à

l'occidentalité en les dépassant au profit d'une synthèse
neuve. (*51*, p.40)

There are, however, points on which Kane does not espouse
entirely the cause of *négritude*. In so far as Samba Diallo is his
mouthpiece, one recalls the latter's rejection of Lucienne's evocation
of his *négritude*: 'J'avoue que je n'aime pas ce mot et que je ne
comprends pas toujours ce qu'il recouvre' (p.155). Speaking in
interview on his own account, Kane is more precise as to what
offends him in the concept:

> Il y a deux aspects qui me gênent dans la Négritude. La
> première c'est ce que Césaire a exprimé de façon
> splendide dans *Le Cahier d'un retour au pays natal* en
> ces termes: 'je revendique pour ma race la louange
> éclatante du crachat'. Je comprends qu'il ait pu dire cela.
> Mais je refuse que le crachat soit une louange. [...] Le
> deuxième aspect, c'est que dans la Négritude, il y a une
> sorte de revendication de l'animisme, or je ne suis pas un
> animiste. (*11*, p.137)

He could have added that, unlike some of the apologists of
négritude, he has no fear of technology. Salif Bâ, in *Les Gardiens du
temple*, is an agronomist, and Kane himself has spent most of his
career in the world of technical development, running even today an
experimental cattle project near the mouth of the Senegal River.

But the hold on tradition is equally fundamental. Without a
clear consciousness of where it comes from, a society cannot go
forward to the future. In the words again of Fougeyrollas:

> Il faut [...] reconnaître que les hommes des sociétés
> contemporaines ont le plus grand besoin, en entrant dans
> cette ère nouvelle, d'être assurés de ce qu'ils ont été et de
> ce qu'ils sont, afin qu'ils puissent devenir *autres* en
> restant, jusqu'à un certain point, *mêmes*. (*51*, p.214)

5. An Ambiguous Death

While the conflict of cultures is clearly the theme around which Cheikh Hamidou Kane constructs his novel from a narrative and philosophical point of view, and which, as far as he is concerned, occupies centre stage, there is a sense in which death is at least as important as a theme, providing a ground-base of imagery and event throughout, and the climax to the narrative. Critics have not been slow in pointing out the crucial role played by death in the novel: Anozie writes of death in *L'Aventure ambiguë* as a 'structure thématique obsessionnelle' (*37*, p.157), while Monnin, interpreting Samba Diallo's death as the end of a 'quête mystique', declares that in introducing this element the author 'a transcendé la problématique de la rencontre des cultures et a donné à son œuvre une dimension universelle dans la mesure où il a traité avant tout de l'angoisse existentielle de l'homme' (*35*, p.53). Is there a conflict between the two themes, too much of a dispersion between the forward-looking attempt to resolve the confrontation of cultures, and the impasse represented by death? Or are the two aspects blended in such a way as to complement and illuminate each other? The mystical texture of the epilogue is certainly only comprehensible in the context of a certain resolution of conflict in death.

What is clear is that death is everywhere in Kane's novel. It opens with a scene of mortification, and closes with the death of the principal character. In between, the philosophical values of death are debated, it is put forward almost as a way of life, and used as image in countless different ways. Samba Diallo's fascination with the idea of death is illustrated, for instance, in the way he visits the tomb of his dead friend, *la Vieille Rella*, and meditates on the significance of her disappearance: 'Longtemps, l'enfant, près de son amie morte, songea à l'éternel mystère de la mort...' (p.53), and concludes she is in Paradise. He makes a significant link with the *foyer ardent* when he continues: 'le Paradis était bâti avec les Paroles qu'il récitait, des mêmes lumières brillantes, des mêmes ombres mystérieuses et profondes, de la même féerie, de la même puissance', and elsewhere admits that fascination with the death of *la Vieille Rella* was of the same order as his devotion to the *foyer ardent* (p.76). This parallel is significant because it is the *foyer ardent* and *le maître* who are the very incarnation of these values of death which so obsess Samba Diallo. If *la Grande Royale* wants to get Samba Diallo away from the Koranic school, it is only partly to save the Diallobé people: it is also because she feels the values represented by *le maître* are unhealthy: 'Cet enfant parle de la mort en termes qui ne sont pas de son âge', she says to *le maître* (p.35). *Le maître* himself is represented from the beginning as close to death. His body no longer obeys him, his calf-muscles are as dry as the dead wood which his disciples burn (p.39). His real, physical death comes as the only logical conclusion to years of self-mortification, to the destruction of the needs of the flesh.

This is the 'positive' side to death, the abandonment of all that hinders the return to the Divine, and the one with which Samba Diallo identifies closely. But there is a negative aspect to death, identified with the death of *le maître*, and illustrated for example when *le fou* says to him: 'Quand tu mourras, toutes ces maisons de paille mourront avec toi' (p.100). The gradual disintegration of the *pays des Diallobé* is thus implicated in what Lemuel A. Johnson calls 'the near-pathological excesses of mortification and ecstasy' (*31*, p.241) to which *le maître* has been committed throughout his long career. The necessary link in the person of *le maître* between the longed-for mystical reunification with the Divine, the death of the non-spiritual, and the lack of development of the *pays des Diallobé* is demonstrated in his inability to go forward. It is this link which *la Grande Royale* wishes to break by sending the Diallobé children to the *école étrangère*.

It seems, however, that Kane wants to underline the position of death in Diallobé society, by indicating in several ways how it differs from the way in which death is regarded in modern times in the West. In the passage just referred to, where we see Samba Diallo in the cemetery, the child is overawed by the mystery of death, but his fear is part of a whole, comprehensive experience. This approach to death, which has nothing morbid about it in fact, is confirmed later in his dialogue with Pierre Louis and his family, where, trying to explain why in Paris he lives 'less fully' than in the *pays des Diallobé*, he says:

> Il me semble qu'au pays des Diallobé l'homme est plus proche de la mort, par exemple. Il vit plus dans sa familiarité. [...] Là-bas, il existait entre elle et moi une intimité, faite tout à la fois de ma terreur et de mon attente. Tandis qu'ici, la mort m'est redevenue une étrangère. Tout le [*sic*] combat, la refoule loin des corps et des esprits. Je l'oublie. Quand je la cherche avec ma pensée, je ne vois qu'un sentiment desséché, une éventualité abstraite... (p.162)

It is doubtless to make a cultural point regarding the fundamental acceptance of death among the Diallobé, that Kane introduces the long set-piece scene where *le maître* recounts the death of *la Grande Royale*'s father, a scene which, by being set back in time, becomes emblematic of the Muslim way to die (pp.36-38). Mbengue reinforces this emblematic quality by making a parallel with one of the accounts of the death of the Prophet (*19*, p.39), and Mamadou Wane, in words which recall Kane's fictionalised account, speaks of the Tokolor, 'dominant de toute sa hauteur la mort [...]. Croyant, il ne peut, à l'heure du "départ" et du "commencement de la fin", que relier sa trajectoire à celle de Dieu, aimé et craint' (*73*, p.386). His whole life is spent in an 'apprentissage de la mort': 'Domestiquant la mort, sans aucun droit à exiger, sans aucune prétention à exhiber, avec au fond de lui cette certitude: le passage ne se fera qu'avec l'aide de Dieu, c'est en définitive ce sentiment religieux qui définit le mieux l'homme toucouleur...' The idea of 'domestiquant la mort' is surely significant, evoking the idea of familiarity experienced by Samba Diallo. That this idea transcends Islam, and is a general phenomenon of the African world-view is illustrated by Mouralis, when (quoting Jacques Maquet), he writes of the way in which '[la mort] n'avait pas le caractère tragique et scandaleux qu'elle revêt dans les traditions individualistes' (*64*, p.81). Kane himself makes the same point when he says, in interview:

La mort est présente – était présente – dans la pratique
religieuse diallobé, musulmane, et aussi, je crois, dans les
pratiques non-musulmanes de ces régions, n'est-ce pas? Il
n'y a pas, dans ce monde-là, cette rupture, cette césure
entre la vie et la mort, entre les morts et les vivants, entre
les ancêtres disparus et les générations vivant
aujourd'hui. Je crois que cela continue à être le cas
encore: la mort est plus présente dans l'esprit et les
préoccupations des gens aujourd'hui, ici, dans nos pays,
qu'elle ne l'est, je crois, dans les préoccupations d'esprit
des gens en Occident... (*16*)

In emphasising the familiarity of death to the Diallobé, what
Johnson calls 'the apocalyptic agony that infuses [Kane's] Sufi
ecstasy' (*31*, p.249) should not be forgotten. It is perhaps best
illustrated in the sunset which forms the back-cloth to the dialogue
between *le Chevalier* and Paul Lacroix. The contrast between the two
world-views is aptly indicated in the language used: what for the
unbeliever Lacroix is simply the setting sun (which will rise again in
the morning) is for *le Chevalier* 'le soleil qui meurt' (p.90), the
anthropomorphism of the image giving it a totally different
resonance. 'Quand le soleil meurt, aucune certitude scientifique ne
doit empêcher qu'on le pleure, aucune évidence rationnelle, qu'on se
demande s'il renaîtra.' This difference of perspective explains also
the perception of *le fou* when he evokes his experience in Europe:
recalling the arid, inhuman, urban landscape he found there, he talks
of 'des espaces mortels [...] des étendues mortelles' (p.104). But this
is death *à l'européenne*, death from which the spirit is absent, a
'dead' death which cannot nourish, unlike the value-charged concept
of death in the *pays des Diallobé*. As Marc, with a nice sense of
irony, comments to Samba Diallo in the course of their conversation
on cultural difference, 'en somme, [...] vous vous plaignez de ne plus
vivre votre mort' (p.162).

    Death is everywhere in this novel, therefore: space precludes an
analysis of its multiple other appearances in the narrative. There
remains, however, its principal manifestation, in the death of Samba
Diallo himself, and it is to this that our attention must now be turned,

since there are many problems surrounding its interpretation. Why should a writer, at the end of what is essentially an autobiographical novel, want to put his principal character to death? Was he simply at a loss to know how to finish the work? Given the sureness of literary touch elsewhere in the novel, it seems unlikely. Does Kane's desire to emphasise the Muslim aspect of the work get the better of him at this point, as El Nouty suggests when he writes: 'Ce qu'on avait pris pour un roman de l'aliénation doit être lu comme une apologétique' (*25*, p.480)? Or is it an echo of the classic death of the Romantic hero, at odds with the world he finds himself in? Critics have evoked also the possibility of his death being a suicide. Adverse criticism has focused on the way in which Samba Diallo's death 'n'éclaire aucun problème général et on peut même se demander si elle résout les problèmes particuliers du héros' (*18*, p.87).

Kane himself has commented on his hero's death on several occasions. In the interview with Maryse Condé, he says:

> Si j'ai fait mettre Samba Diallo à mort, c'était un peu pour souligner l'aspect dramatique et tragique de cette aventure intellectuelle et spirituelle qui est la nôtre, à nous tous les Africains, partant de notre société et allant vers la modernité et vers les civilisations et des systèmes de valeurs différents des nôtres. (*10*)

And again, 'Je voulais seulement montrer que ce voyage est difficile' (*26*, p.VII). More recently, he has stated that:

> La manière dont Samba Dialla meurt est un témoignage de sa conviction que la mort physique ne met pas un terme à tout, il y a un au-delà où quelques-unes des contradictions qu'on a vécues ici-bas, disparaissent, parce qu'elles sont relatives au fait qu'on est vivant, mais au regard de Dieu, au regard du Créateur, ce qui peut paraître comme contradiction chez nous est quelque chose qui ne l'est pas. (*16*)

This would underline the apologetic nature of the hero's death, where death is seen as not so much an escape as the only locus in which contradictions are seen for what they really are. In the same interview, however, we have already seen how, in a reinterpretation of the role of *le fou*, he declares Samba Diallo's death to be a warning against fundamentalist Islam: the young man dies at the hand of a fanatic, who wishes to impose upon another person the obligation to pray at a certain time, while Samba Diallo himself refuses this imposition as being against the true spirit of Islam. His death is thus the result of a 'malentendu', 'un accident stupide' (*16*).

It would seem that no single explanation is possible without impoverishing the text. In the circumstances, the wisest course would seem to be to return to the oral tradition which can so often, as we have seen, throw light on this text. Hampâté Bâ, in one of his many presentations of these literatures, emphasises that when it comes to 'textes initiatiques', many different levels of interpretation are possible, depending on the level of understanding of the audience. In this way, the same account can be understood by both child and initiate (*41*, p. 86). A multiple reading of this aspect of *L'Aventure ambiguë* is equally rewarding.

On a purely narrative level, then, Samba Diallo's death, as we have just seen, is the result of a misunderstanding: *le fou* interprets his 'Non... je n'accepte pas', addressed to a God who refuses to reveal himself, as a refusal to pray, and in his desperation at what he takes to be Samba Diallo's apostasy, takes out his weapon and kills him. It is an accident, albeit caused directly by contact with the West, which has both confused Samba Diallo and deranged *le fou*. It can thus be read as a condemnation of Western influence.

Is it a suicide? Anozie would tend to think so, since death is essentially 'voulu'. It is a 'sublimation de la psychose, obsession dont Samba Diallo est victime dès le début' (*37*, p.156). And it is true that in this final passage, Samba Diallo has already evoked the possibility of his death: 'Peut-être, après tout. Contraindre Dieu... Lui donner le choix, entre son retour dans votre cœur, ou votre mort, au nom de Sa gloire' (p.187). But on a narrative level, Samba Diallo can have no idea that *le fou* is about to kill him, and so can hardly be said to be offering himself up as sacrificial victim. And in the passage just quoted, the principal idea is the return of God into his heart – one way or another. Clearly here speaking as a devout Muslim (why else would he talk of 'Sa gloire'?), he would know that death offers reconciliation with God. He is desperate, but desperate for the unity with which he was familiar in his childhood, rather than for death. Kane himself is resolutely against the idea of Samba Diallo's death being a suicide, maintaining at the same time that the latter had not lost his religious faith: 'Beaucoup de personnes ont pensé que Samba Diallo avait en quelque sorte suscité son meurtre par le fou, parce qu'il avait abouti à une impasse, qu'il voulait se suicider. D'autres ont pensé et dit que Samba Diallo avait perdu la foi. Je ne partage pas ces opinions, ni l'une ni l'autre' (*16*). On the other hand, as we have seen, in the same interview he speaks of death as being 'peut-être une manière de résoudre les problèmes dont on n'avait pas trouvé la solution ici-bas'. But it is clear for Kane, here and in the other passages quoted, that life and death form a sort of continuum, and the idea of voluntary death as 'putting an end to it all' makes little sense in the context of the novel.

On an autobiographical level, one could make the point that Samba Diallo's death is the liquidation of that part of Cheikh Hamidou Kane which, like the condemned Diallobé society, had no place in the future. The mystical contemplative 'qui eût dû naître contemporain de ses ancêtres' (p.133) is simply not equipped to confront the aggression of the Western world, and the future belongs to the likes of Demba. One might take the point further and ask, in psychoanalytical mode, if it is not the putting to death of his father's dream for him: we know that Kane was destined for the Koranic school, whereas it was his elder brother who was destined for *l'école étrangère* (*6*). The colonial authorities having decided differently, it was essential for Kane to exorcise this particular dream before he could engage in a career in development administration with peace of mind.

Kane's own interpretation of how things might have worked out had Samba Diallo not died is very different. As we saw in the opening chapter, he considers that, if *le fou* had not assassinated him, his hero would have gone on to explain to the Diallobé 'comment lier le bois au bois', he would have helped them towards a better future by revealing the secrets of the West which he had learned (this is the view of Samba Diallo we have in *Les Gardiens du temple*). However, it seems much more appropriate to charge, not Samba Diallo, but Cheikh Hamidou Kane himself, and Samba Diallo's reincarnation, Salif Bâ in *Les Gardiens du temple*, with this role, a role for which they are both admirably fitted.

Looking at Samba Diallo's death from a sociological perspective, it seems that it represents the end of *la Grande Royale*'s hopes, not for Diallobé society as such (Demba is there to assure a pragmatic vision for the future, and some sort of alliance between the faith represented by *le foyer ardent* and the technological society represented by *l'école étrangère* seems assured), but for the ruling *toorodbe* society for which she stands. The aristocracy will not be the first or the only ones to benefit from the coloniser's secrets. In the struggle between *la Grande Royale* and *le maître*, paradoxically *le maître* wins, although he is already dead. If we accept, as Kane does, the total unity of purpose between traditional Diallobé society and Islam, then it is these traditional values, those of death, which are upheld by Samba Diallo's assassination. As Mbye B. Cham puts it, 'His death, far from implying the defeat of Diallobé Islamic doctrine, vindicates its view of the ephemerality of mortal existence and the primacy of the spiritual' (*46*, p.169).

A mystical interpretation such as this, whereby death is seen as a liberation of the spirit, has the merit of taking account of the epilogue, which otherwise might seem to be something of an indulgence. Samba Diallo finds his accomplishment in death and after death, where all contradiction and ambiguity are resolved. It also picks up the important theme of initiation, and makes sense of it both from the point of view of Sufi mysticism (Samba Diallo's early training) and the initiation *à rebours* which he undergoes in Europe. Death is the necessary door to life, but a life immeasurably fuller than the one he is leaving. Samba Diallo's search for the lost paradise of his childhood leads him in fact to ultimate reality. The suffering which precedes his death is a classic feature of all mysticism, and is part of the initiation process (in Sufi terms, the *jihad* of purification, the greater 'holy war' against the baseness of one's own soul) (see *38*, p.157). The knowledge conveyed by initiation is always dangerous, always accompanied by the possibility of death (*71*, p.63), although the 'death' of the soul is not necessarily a physical one, and a possible reading of what happens to Samba Diallo can at least downplay the idea of literal, physical death, if only because the writer is concentrating on a metaphysical continuum where boundaries are unclear. The ecstasy following 'death' is as real in terms of *fanâ'*, the mystical vision of the Infinite (see above, p.32) as in the after-life. The greatest suffering is occasioned by the sense of isolation, of disorientation, and in particular of the absence of God, the 'dark night of the soul', as John of the Cross termed it, when the soul feels abandoned by God. This is Samba Diallo's experience as, confronted by *le fou* with his formalistic demands that no longer seem to make any sense, he tries desperately to enter into communion with his God. His 'dark night' is provoked by his contact with the materialism of the West, and with the rootless intellectualism he found there.

Had Samba Diallo lost his religious faith at this point? There is no doubt that he was deeply disorientated. He addresses *le maître*, now dead, wishing longingly that he were there to tell him what to believe: 'Je ne crois plus grand-chose, de ce que tu m'avais appris. Je ne sais pas ce que je crois'. But, as if admitting his limitations as a human being, he adds: 'Mais l'étendue est tellement immense de ce que je ne sais pas, et qu'il faut bien que je croie' (p.186). Kane himself, as we have already noted, does not believe that Samba Diallo has lost his faith, and this would be borne out by the fact that he continues to address God to the end. The reality of God's presence is hidden from him, for reasons which he does not understand, but that does not prove his lack of existence. Samba Diallo's last words are a proof of his continuing belief against the evidence: 'Tu ne saurais m'oublier comme cela. Je n'accepterai pas, seul de nous deux, de pâtir de Ton éloignement. Je n'accepterai pas. Non...' (p.187). One does not, after all, address a non-existent being.[3]

---

[3] One is reminded of the words Beckett puts into the mouth of Clov in *Endgame*: indignant at the lack of response to his attempt to pray to God, he blurts out: 'The bastard! He doesn't exist!'

In whatever way we choose to interpret the death of Samba Diallo – and we would contend that several approaches are necessary to grasp the significance of the event in all its complexity – it is clear that it forms the logical climax to a novel which is shot through with the theme of death from start to finish. It is in death that the ambiguities and paradoxes of the novel find their fullest expression. Starting in mortification, the novel ends in ecstasy, but it is an ecstasy which is truly a function of that mortification, and could not exist without it. It is in this ground-bass of death, but a concept of death that does not put an end to everything, that the epilogue (pp.188-91) finds its justification: unlike the epilogue of the realist tradition, which fulfils the function of tying up the loose ends of the action, revealing the current situation of the characters, sometimes many years later, the epilogue of *L'Aventure ambiguë*, in an ultimate expression of the omniscient narrator, is concerned with establishing a continuation of the spirit beyond death, in a breakdown of time and space. Located in a place beyond place, which can only be conveyed through images of universality such as the sea, and where time exists only as an 'instant qui dure', where all oppositions are abolished, the Word which has been the vehicle of partial reality to Samba Diallo during his life finds its final revelation in the Voice which greets him, a Voice which is 'annonciateur de fin d'exil'. It is significant that the Voice has no physical form, and that the entire epilogue consists only of dialogue, of voices responding antiphonally one to another.

The epilogue thus marks the end, outside time and space, of the exile to which Samba Diallo was subject in life. In fact, his was a double and paradoxical exile (see *34*): on a simple, narrative level, he leaves his home for exile in the West, first through its schooling, and then more literally in Paris. And exile is painful, because it cuts him off from the paradise of his childhood. But this paradise is represented by another form of exile, evident from the very first pages of the novel: in the *foyer ardent*, his Sufi training is aimed at exiling him from the materiality of this world. He is, paradoxically, a soul *striving for* exile, the exile which is his true spiritual home, and which he finds only in the climax to his adventure. An ambiguous adventure indeed, exceeding the narrow bounds of mere autobiography to explore the inner world of anguish and loss, the conflicting demands of the spiritual and the material, confronted with a wider world destined to remain problematic.

Conclusion

L'Aventure ambiguë is the statement of a dilemma which is not resolved within the novel. Beyond the conflict of cultures around which the debate of the novel revolves, there is an even more fundamental dilemma, referring to the death-theme which was evoked in the previous chapter, which can be expressed thus: how can one separate the 'positive' aspect of death, representing the mystical tradition, 'l'ombre' which the world thirsts for, as *le Chevalier* says, and which Kane identifies with Diallobé values, from the 'negative', the decay and despair of under-development which is destroying the Diallobé and which, paradoxically, will destroy the 'positive' aspect, as material wretchedness makes people desert their traditional faith? The two perspectives on death are fused in *le maître*, who thereby confesses his inability to help the Diallobé forward. *La Grande Royale* courageously confronts the issue, but her strategy also fails: her chosen emissary, Samba Diallo, is also unable to resolve the dilemma, *becoming*, in fact, that dilemma.

In one sense, the novel could be called 'an elegy for the Diallobé'. Samba Diallo, in his recitation during *la nuit du Coran*, is conscious of the ending of an era, and of the significance of that moment: he is aware of his particular responsibility to play his part *well*. And it is right and proper that the old Diallobé society should be mourned, and that all the resources of language should be enlisted to sing its passing. *L'Aventure ambiguë* is conceived in tragic mode – the narrator, justifying his unwillingness to elaborate on the joyful moments of Samba Diallo and his little playmates in school, speaks of 'ce récit dont la vérité profonde est toute de tristesse' (p.62). In consequence the language used to convey this sadness will be devoid of exuberance: discreet, impersonal, universalising in tendency.

But the elegiac sadness is shot through with anguish at the uncertainty of what is to replace this dying world. How can one 'save' at one and the same time the God of the *foyer ardent* and the dying houses of the Diallobé? The only solutions offered to resolve the dilemma are muted, and put in the mouth of a character (*le Chevalier*), who shares his son's anguish, or are outside the novel itself – projected either into real life, or into Kane's subsequent novel, *Les Gardiens du temple*. But it is not the primary function of literature to provide solutions to the problems of society. It can happen, sometimes almost incidentally, and the primary literary function retained; but the most memorable moments in literature tend to reflect the problems in all their stark reality, rather than the solutions. Samba Diallo living 'happily ever after' would have little interest for the reader. But in his account of his hero's ill-fated journey from the *pays des Diallobé* to the *pays des Blancs* and back, Cheikh Hamidou Kane has succeeded in marrying many of the devices of the African oral tradition with universal archetypal patterns of death, rebirth, journey, quest, adventure, the whole couched in a language of a singular beauty, to create a synthesis which, in its use of paradox and ambiguity, is entirely new. In it he goes beyond the initial, partially autobiographical, and limited situation of his hero, to make a statement of witness which is universal in its challenge as in its implications.

Select Bibliography

Unless otherwise stated, Paris is the place of publication for works published in France. Cheikh Hamidou Kane is here abbreviated to CHK, *L'Aventure ambiguë* to *AA* (after the first item) and the Institut Fondamental d'Afrique Noire at Dakar to IFAN.

A. WRITINGS BY CHEIKH HAMIDOU KANE

NOVELS

1. *L'Aventure ambiguë*, Préface de Vincent Monteil, Julliard, 1961; paperback edition referred to in this volume: UGE, Coll. 10/18, 1971, Dakar: NEA – Yaoundé: CLE, 1980
2. *Les Gardiens du temple*, Stock, 1995

ARTICLES, PREFACES ETC.

3. 'Comme si nous nous étions donné rendez-vous' (communication faite au Colloque de Royaumont), *Esprit* (octobre 1961), 375-87
4. 'Plan National et l'option sénégalaise de développement socialiste'. Discours prononcé au Colloque sur les politiques de développement et les diverses voies africaines du socialisme, Dakar, décembre 1962 (unpublished)
5. 'Préface' à Simone Kaya, *Les Danseuses d'Impé-Eya, jeunes filles à Abidjan*, Abidjan: INADES, 1976

INTERVIEWS

6. 'Une Aventure ambiguë', television/video interview with CHK, France-Télévision, *Espaces Francophones*, 1997
7. 'CHK: de *AA* aux *Gardiens du temple*', interview with Boubacar Boris Diop, *Démocraties* [Dakar], n.s. 7 (février 1996), 6, 7 & 11
8. 'CHK: le devoir de fidélité', in Lise Gauvin, *Ecrivains francophones à la croisée des langues: entretiens*, Karthala, 1997, pp. 139-52
9. 'CHK: le devoir de vigilance' (entretien avec Noël X. Ebony), *Africa* [Dakar], 170 (mars 1985), 81-83

10. 'CHK répond à Maryse Condé', disque édité par CLEF-ORTF, 1974

11. '*Les Gardiens du temple* ou l'invention d'une "modernité traditionnelle": entretien avec CHK', propos recueillis par Boniface Mongo-Mboussa et Babacar Sall, *Sociétés Africaines et Diaspora*, 5 (janvier 1997), 129-38

12. ITW Africa No. 1 (1996) [cassette loaned by CHK]

13. 'Monsieur CHK est interviewé par le Professeur Barthélémy Kotchy', *Etudes Littéraires*, VII, 3 (déc. 1974), 479-86

14. RFI (Mémoires d'un continent, 1995) [cassette loaned by CHK]

15. RTI (Panorama International) [cassette loaned by CHK]

16. With J. P. Little, Dakar, 16 December 1997 (published in part under the title 'The origins of Samba Diallo: An Interview with Cheikh Hamidou Kane' in the *International Journal of Francophone Studies*, II, 2 [1999], 112-20)

WRITINGS ON CHEIKH HAMIDOU KANE

BOOKS AND THESES

17. Battestini, Monique et Simon, & Roger Mercier, *AA*, Nathan, 1964.

18. Getrey, Jean, *Comprendre AA de CHK*, Editions Saint-Paul, Les Classiques Africains, 1982

19. Mbengue, Ndiaga Younousse, 'CHK romancier', Mémoire de Maîtrise, Lettres Modernes, Dakar: U.C.A.D., 1980-81

20. Moriceau, Annie, & Alain Rouch, *AA de CHK*, Nathan/Dakar: Nouvelles Editions Africaines, 1983. Contains extracts from *10*

21. Tine, Alioune, 'Etude de la métaphore et de la métonymie dans *AA* de CHK', Thesis, Université de Lyon II, 1976

ARTICLES

22. Calin, William, 'Between two worlds: the Quest for Death and Life in CHK's *AA*', *Kentucky Romance Quarterly*, XIX, 2, 183-97

23. Chartier, Monique L., 'L'eau et le feu dans *AA* de CHK', *Présence Francophone*, 9 (1974), 15-25

24. Diop, Boubacar Boris, 'Les métamorphoses de Samba Diallo', *Présence Africaine*, 153 (1er trimestre 1996), 197-205

25. El Nouty, Hassan, 'La polysémie de *AA*', *Revue de Littérature Comparée*, 191-192 (1974), 475-87

26. Fottorino, Eric, 'Hamidou Kane: la "torche noire"', *Le Monde [des Livres]* (9 février 1996), VII

27. Gadgigo, Samba, 'Literature and History: the case of *AA* by CHK', *Bridges: A Senegalese Journal of English Studies* [Dakar], 3 (1er semestre 1991), 31-40

28. Goré, Jeanne-Lydie, 'Le thème de la solitude dans *AA* de CHK', *Actes du Colloque sur la littérature africaine d'expression française, Dakar, 26-29 mars 1963*, Dakar: Faculté des Lettres et Sciences Humaines, Langues et Littératures, 14 (1965), 177-88

29. Hale, Jane Alison, 'Reading, writing and schooling in CHK's *Ambiguous Adventure*' [unpublished; copy communicated to me by CHK]

30. Harrow, Kenneth W., 'Camara Laye, CHK and Tayeb Salib: Three Sufi Authors', in *54*, pp. 261-97

31. Johnson, Lemuel A., 'Crescent and Consciousness: Islamic Orthodoxies and the West African Novel', in *54*, pp. 239-60

32. Kane, Fadel, 'Société, culture et mutations dans *La Maison au figuier* d'Abdoulaye Elimane Kane', Projet de thèse de doctorat 3e cycle, Faculté des Lettres et Sciences Humaines, Université de Dakar (unpublished)

33. Little, J. P., 'The Context of *AA*: Aspects of the School System in *L'Afrique Occidentale Française*', *ASCALF Bulletin*, 6 (Spring-Summer 1993), 10-27

34. —, 'The Dialogue of Exile: CHK's *AA*', in *Exiles and Migrants: Crossing Thresholds in European Culture and Society*, ed. Anthony Coulson, Brighton: Sussex Academic Press, 1977, pp. 136-43

35. Monnin, Edith, 'La quête mystique de Samba Diallo', *Revue de Littérature et d'Esthétique Africaines*, 4 (1982), 43-53

36. Simon, P.-H., '*AA*', *Le Monde* (26.7.61)

BACKGROUND MATERIAL

RELEVANT LITERARY AND CULTURAL STUDIES

37. Anozie, Sunday O., *Sociologie du roman africain*, Aubier-Montaigne, 1970

38. Asfar, Denise, '*Kaïdara*: Islam and Traditional Religion in a West African Narrative of Initiation', in *54*, pp. 151-61

39. Bâ, Amadou Hampâté, 'Culture peule', Intervention au 1er Congrès international des écrivains et artistes noirs, Paris-Sorbonne, 19-22 sept. 1956, *Présence Africaine*, n. s., 8-10 (juin-nov. 1956), 85-97

40. —, *Kaïdara: rite initiatique peul*, ed. Lilyan Kesteloot, Julliard, 1968

41.—, *Petit Bodiel, conte drolatique peul*, Abidjan: Nouvelles Editions Ivoiriennes, 1993

42. — & G. Dieterlen (trad. et comm.), *Koumen, texte initiatique des pasteurs peuls*, Paris/The Hague: Mouton, 1961

43. —, Lilyan Kesteloot, Christiane Seydou & Alfâ Ibrâhîm Sow (eds), *L'Eclat de la grande étoile suivi de Bain rituel: récits initiatiques peuls de Amadou Hampâté Bâ*, Armand Colin, Classiques Africains, 1974

44. Bol, Victor, 'Les formes du roman africain', *Actes du Colloque sur la littérature africaine d'expression française, Dakar, 26-29 mars 1963*, Dakar: Faculté des Lettres et Sciences Humaines, Langues et Littératures, 14 (1965), 133-38

45. Calame-Griaule, Geneviève, 'L'Art de la parole dans la culture africaine', *Présence Africaine*, 47 (3ᵉ trimestre 1963), 74-79

46. Cham, Mbye B., 'Islam in Senegalese Literature and Film', in *54*, pp. 163-86

47. Chevrier, Jacques, *Littérature africaine*, Hatier, 1990

48. Coulon, Christian, 'Pouvoir oligarchique et mutations sociales et politiques au Fouta Toro', in J.-L. Balans, C. Coulon, J.-M. Gastellu, *Autonomie locale et intégration nationale au Sénégal*, Pédone, 1975

49. Corbin, Henri, *Avicenne et le récit visionnaire*, I: *Etude sur le cycle des récits aviciens*, Téhéran: Dépt d'Iranologie de l'Institut franco-iranien, Paris: Librairie d'Amérique et d'Orient Adrien-Maisonneuve, 1954

50. Diop, Abdoulaye Bara, *Société toucouleur et migration*, Dakar: IFAN, Initiations et Etudes, XVIII (1965)

51. Fougeyrollas, Pierre, *Modernisation des hommes: l'exemple du Sénégal*, Flammarion, 1967

52. Frobenius, Leo, *Histoire de la civilisation africaine*, trans. H. Back & D. Ermont, Gallimard, 1933

53. Hardy, Georges, *Une Conquête morale: l'enseignement en A.O.F.*, Armand Colin, 1917

54. Harrow, Kenneth W., ed., *Faces of Islam in African Literature*, Portsmouth, NH: Heinemann, London: James Currey, 1991

55. Jahn, J., *Muntu, l'homme africain et la culture néo-africaine*, trans. Brian de Martinoir, Seuil, 1951

56. Kane, Issa, 'L'enfant toucouleur', *Bulletin de l'enseignement de l'A.O.F.* (1931-32)

57. Kane, Mohamadou, 'Sur les "formes traditionnelles" du roman africain', *Annales de la Faculté des Lettres et Sciences Humaines de Dakar*, 5 (1975), 7-38

58. Leusse, Hubert de, *Afrique et Occident. Heurs et malheurs d'une rencontre*, Editions de l'Orante, 1971

59. Lings, Martin, *What is Soufism?*, London: George Allen and Unwin, 1975

60. Ly, Boubacar, 'L'honneur dans les sociétés Ouolof et Toucouleur du Sénégal', *Présence Africaine*, 61 (1ᵉʳ trimestre 1967), 32-67

61. Mbiti, John, *African Religions and Philosophy*, London, Ibadan, Nairobi: Heinemann, 1969

62. Monteil, Vincent, 'Contribution à la sociologie des Peuls (Le "Fonds Vieillard" de l'IFAN)', *Bulletin de l'IFAN*, XXXII, série B, no. 3 (1970)

63. —, *L'Islam noir*, Seuil, 1980

64. Mouralis, Bernard, 'Individu et collectivité dans le roman négro-africain d'expression française', *Annales de l'Université d'Abidjan*, Série D – Lettres, no, 2 (1969)

65. —, *Littérature et développement*, Champion, 1981

66. Nadjo, Léon, 'Langue française et identité culturelle en Afrique francophone', *Ethiopiques*, III, 1-2 (1er trimestre 1985), 94-105

67. Robinson, David, 'An Approach to Islam in West African History', in *54*, pp. 107-29

68. —, *Chiefs and Clerics: Abdul Bokar Kane and Futa Toro 1853-1891*, Oxford: Clarendon Press, 1975

69. Senghor, Léopold Sédar, 'La Négritude est un humanisme du XXe siècle', in *Liberté 3: Négritude et civilisation de l'universel*, Seuil, 1977, pp. 69-79

70. —, 'Négritude et modernité ou la négritude est un humanisme du XXe siècle', in *Liberté 3: Négritude et civilisation de l'universel*, Seuil, 1977, pp. 215-242

71. Sow, Ibrahima, 'Le Monde peul à travers le mythe du berger céleste', *Ethiopiques* [Dakar], 19 (juillet 1979), 49-69

72. Touré, El Hadj Seydou Nourou, 'Société, pouvoir et régime foncier au Fuuta Tooro (Sénégal) dans la première moitié du XIXe siècle', *Bulletin de l'IFAN*, XLVI, 1-2 (1984-85), 115-36

73. Wane, Mamadou, 'Réflexions sur la dimension sacrale chez les Toucouleurs', *Bulletin de l'IFAN*, XXXXIX, B, 2 (1977), 386-404

74. Wane, Yaya, 'Besoins sociaux et mobilité des Toucouleurs', *Notes Africaines* [Dakar: IFAN], 101 (janvier 1964), 16-24

75. —, *Les Toucouleurs du Fouta Tooro (Sénégal), Stratification sociale et structure familiale*, Dakar: IFAN, Initiations et Etudes, XVIII (1965)

76. —, 'Les Toucouleurs du Sénégal et la modernisation', *Bulletin de l'IFAN*, XXXII, série B, no. 3 (1970), 888-900

77. Zahan, Dominique, *Religion, spiritualité et pensée africaines*, Payot, 1970

OTHER RELEVANT NOVELS IN FRENCH

78. Badian, Seydou, *Sous l'orage*, Présence Africaine, 1963

79. Camara, Laye, *L'Enfant noir*, Plon, 1953

80. Kane, Abdoulaye Elimane, *La Maison au figuier*, Dakar: Nouvelles Editions Africaines, Saint-Maur: Sépia, 1994

81. Lam, Aboubacry Moussa, *La Fièvre de la terre*, L'Harmattan, 1991.

82. Loba, Aké, *Kokoumba, l'étudiant noir*, Flammarion, 1960

83. Mudimbe, V. Y., *L'Ecart*, Présence Africaine, 1979

84. Socé, Ousmane, *Mirages de Paris*, Nouvelles Editions Latines, 1937